The GREAT FAMINE

The GREAT FAMINE
IRELAND'S POTATO FAMINE
—— 1845–51 ——

John Percival

Foreword by Ian Gibson

Viewer Books

New York

ACKNOWLEDGEMENTS

This book is intended to bring the story of a tragic period in Irish history to a large number of readers who may not be familiar with the detailed background to the catastrophe. I refer those who wish to investigate the facts more deeply to the select bibliography and the notes at the back of this book. I have made use of all of these words in one way or another, but my greatest debt is to the economic historian, Cormac O'Grada, whose detailed evaluation of the famine and its causes extends to a large number of scholarly papers in addition to the publications quoted in this book. I have also drawn on interviews with the historians Mary Daly, Christine Kinealy and Roy Foster, as well as the published works of theirs which I have listed.

In the course of my research for the A&E television series on the Great Famine, which prompted this book in the first place, I have also talked to dozens of historians, both professional and amateur, in Ireland, Britain, Canada and the United States. I would like to single out for special thanks several people who went far beyond the usual courtesies in offering their help. These include Fr Patrick Hickey and Padraig de Barra in Ireland, Andre Charbonneau and Marianna O'Gallagher in Quebec, Peter Toner and Harold Wright in Saint John, Denis Noel in Fredericton, Larry Kirwan and Peter Quinn in New York.

I would also like to thank Michael Casey for his research of some primary sources and his timely remarks on the first draft of this book, and finally my colleague and friend, Ian Gibson, who also made some very helpful comments about a number of passages in the first draft. However, where I have stuck my neck out and insisted on keeping ti there, I have only myself to blame. Notwithstanding all this valuable assistance, any errors, and most of the more controversial opinions, are my own.—

John Percival

This is a Viewer Book
Published by TV Books, Inc.
1995

All rights reserved under international and pan-American copyright conventions.

Published in the United States by TV Books, Inc.
1995 Broadway
New York, NY 10023

Distributed to the trade by Penguin USA, New York.
Original edition published in the United Kingdom by BBC Books

Publisher's Cataloging-in-Publication Data
Percival, John.
    The great famine: Ireland's potato famine, 1845–1851 / John Percival; foreword by Ian Gibson.
    p. cm
    Includes bibliographical references and index.
    ISBN 1-57500-002-4.

    1. Ireland—History—1837-1901.   2. Famines—Ireland—History.

    I. Title
    DA950.7.P47 1995   940.5'081   QB195-20393

Picture research by Dierdre O'Day
Printed and bound in Great Britain by Butler & Tanner Ltd
Color separations and jacket printing by Lawrence Allen Ltd

This book is published to accompany the television series entitled *The Great Famine*
produced by BBC and first broadcast in 1995

CONTENTS

FOREWORD

*T*he disease first struck, unevenly, in the autumn of 1845, as if testing its strength. It returned, as a devastation, the following summer. Overnight whole fields turned totally rotten, the stink of pestilential tubers fouling the air. Completely dependent on the potato, one of nature's most versatile foods, the Irish peasantry began to starve. Science could only offer hypotheses to explain the dire visitation, and the one accepted by Westminster – that it was a kind of wet rot – proved incorrect. Too late the killer was identified as a fungus that responded to spraying with a solution of copper sulphate mixed with lime. The blight eventually received a fancy Latin name: *Phytophthora infestans*. In the course of three years it wreaked havoc on Ireland. We will never know the exact figures, but historians tend to agree that about a million people died of starvation and sickness and that a further one-and-a-half million had emigrated by 1851. This out of a total population of about eight million. We are talking about one of the greatest human tragedies of the nineteenth century.

Although Ireland had become an integral part of the United Kingdom in 1801, in practice it remained the same English colony that, since the final defeat of the Celtic chieftains two hundred years earlier, had been consistently bullied and exploited by its more powerful neighbour. The English not only considered the Irish feckless, improvident, ridiculous and excessively voluble, but also inherently untrustworthy. They were rebellious and Catholic as well. All in all, a downright nuisance. Naturally, therefore, when the potato blight hit, and persisted, there was a willingness to believe that the Irish had brought it upon themselves and should be helped as little as possible.

Before we judge the English handling of the Irish famine too harshly, it is important to remember that the men who took the decisions, or failed to take them, were victims of an educational system whose harshness was unparalleled in the so-called civilized world. The public schools instilled stiff-upper-lipped attitudes in which compassion and tenderness were taboo. As boarding schools, they took possession of their charges very young; *in loco parentis* meant 'spare the rod and spoil the child'; and the pupils, having been beaten and humiliated, were allowed, as seniors, to beat and humiliate in turn. Naturally, when those who survived the system attained positions of power in the outside world, this conditioning meant they did not hurry to show pity to other people, at home or abroad (and abroad meant a vast empire). I will be told, of course, that this is a gross generalization and exaggeration. But I do not feel that it is. The bodies of English schoolboys have not, until very recently, been inviolable. This, in my opinion, is a shameful record.

Charles Trevelyan, who was in charge of Irish famine relief under both the Whigs and Tories, has not, I think, yet been the subject of close biographical investigation. Certainly he deserves to be (it would be interesting, among other things, to know how he fared at Charterhouse). Trevelyan talks about the Irish famine as some Christian fundamentalists today refer to AIDS, hinting that here we have an example of how God corrects the ways of his errant children. With the famine, he wrote, 'the deep and inveterate root' of Ireland's ills 'has been laid bare by a direct stroke of an all-wise and all-merciful Providence'. And again: 'Unless we are much deceived, posterity will trace up to that famine the commencement of a salutary revolution in the habits of a nation long singularly unfortunate, and will acknowledge that on this, as on many other occasions, Supreme Wisdom has educed permanent good out of transient evil.' *Note* 'long singularly unfortunate'. Having penned such a trite phrase, Trevelyan does not consider the possibility that one of the most unfortunate things about Ireland might conceivably be its propinquity to the larger, belligerent island lying to the east.

While the great wealth of the Anglican Church was not mustered to help Ireland in her desperate need (nor, signally, was that of the Church of Rome), there were other Christian bodies in Britain which did not pass by on the other side. Both the Quakers and the British Association come out of the famine with great credit. The record of the former is particularly admirable. Free of cloying dogma, the Quakers, working in close unison with their Irish counterparts, did their utmost to get practical help quickly to the places where it was most needed. Their reports, so sensible, so incisive and so redolent of indignation, constitute a telling indictment of Westminster's handling of the tragedy.

It is also true that many individual Church of Ireland (Anglican) ministers did much heroic work alongside their Catholic colleagues, with priests of both persuasions dying in the process; and that the civil servants involved with the famine at ground level often behaved with profound humanity, expressing extreme irritation and even outrage at the Government's lack of generosity and concern. A case in point was Captain Arthur Kennedy, whose strenuous labours on behalf of the inhabitants of Kilrush are recalled in this book.

As presenter of the BBC2 series *The Great Famine,* I have found working with John Percival a considerable privilege, and can vouch for his continuous struggle to be fair to all those involved in the terrible events we are now remembering, 150 years later. That fairness characterizes the present book, where, despite the author's evident dislike of Trevelyan, Sir Charles Wood and others of their ilk, we are invited to consider the context in which they operated and the prejudices and assumptions they assimilated from the society in which they moved, and of which they were characteristic products.

'You can't take the pain out of history!' exclaimed Don Mullan, director of the Irish charity Afri, inspired by the Great Famine, when we interviewed him on a march in remembrance of the victims. He was thinking, perhaps, of certain 'revisionist' attitudes which seem almost to suggest that no one was to blame for what happened. I agree: history's pain should never be forgotten. And it can be put to constructive use. As a nation, the Irish have been remarkably generous in forgiving the English for the suffering inflicted on them over so many centuries. Such magnanimity is a magnificent achievement for, God knows, they have reason enough to be bitter. But the Irish have gone further than this: today the country, its population halved since the famine, is one of those that does most to help people in distress around the world. As a Dubliner of Protestant extraction, brought up largely in ignorance of the famine, I cannot but admire, and reflect on, this further triumph. Hopefully both the series and John Percival's cogent and moving book will serve to stir the historical conscience of England and to remind all of us that, where man's indifference to the sufferings of others is concerned, history has much to teach us about the contemporary world.

Ian Gibson

INTRODUCTION

*B*eing aware that I would have to witness scenes of frightful hunger, I provided myself with as much bread as five men could carry, and on reaching the spot, I was surprised to find the wretched hamlet apparently deserted. I entered some of the hovels to ascertain the cause, and the scenes which presented themselves were such as no tongue or pen can convey the slightest idea of. In the first, six famished and ghastly skeletons, to all appearances dead, were huddled in a corner on some filthy straw, their sole covering what seemed a ragged horsecloth, their wretched legs hanging about, naked above the knees. I approached with horror, and found by low moaning that they were still alive – they were in fever, four children, a woman, and what had once been a man. It is impossible to go through the detail. Suffice it to say, that in a few minutes, I was surrounded by at least 200 such phantoms, such frightful spectres as no words can describe, [suffering] either from famine or from fever. Their demoniac yells are still ringing in my ears and their horrible images are fixed upon my brain.

Part of a letter from Mr Nicholas Cummins, magistrate, to the Duke of Wellington, published in The Times *on Christmas Eve, 1846.*

In six terrible years between 1845 and 1851, over a million Irish men, women and children died from the effects of prolonged hunger and disease. They died in the hovels where they lived, in the workhouses and fever hospitals, in the streets of the towns and in the ditches and bogs of the countryside. They died of starvation, of dysentery, of typhus and relapsing fever, of hypothermia brought on by exposure to wind and rain. The corpses in some places were so numerous that they were loaded on to carts and dumped coffinless into pits. In remoter areas the dead were never buried; their bodies rotted into the earth or were torn to pieces by dogs.

Hundreds of thousands of people were evicted from their homes and left to wander the country roads or drift into the towns, looking hopelessly for food.

Ireland

IN 1848

Malin Head

INISHOWEN

Dunfanaghy
• Gweedore

• Letterkenny

LONDONDERRY
• LONDONDERRY

DONEGAL

U L S T E R

ANTRIM

• BELFAST

Lurgan
•
• Lisburn
Lisburn

DOWN

FERMANAGH

Belmullet
Killala •
Ballina •
Crossmolina

SLIGO •

SLIGO

L E I T R I M

ARMAGH
MONAGHAN
MONAGHAN

CAVAN

MAYO
Newport
CASTLEBAR

C O N N A U G H T

Strokestown

Achill Island
Clare Island • Westport
Louisburgh •
Killary Harbour Doo Lough

R O S C O M M O N

MEATH

River Boyne
• Drogheda

Connemara

GALWAY

KINGS COUNTY

L E I N S T E R

Maynooth •

DUBLIN
•
DUBLIN

River Shannon

• Parsonstown

Ennistymon •

CLARE

CARLOW

Kilkee •
• Kilrush

River Shannon

Thurles •

TIPPERARY
• Cashel

WEXFORD
×
• Vinegar Hill

Mullinahone

Dingle •
Valentia •

KERRY

M U N S T E R

WATERFORD

CORK

CORK
•

Kinsale
•

• Bantry
Schull • Skibbereen
BANTRY BAY

Over a million people – those who could scrape together enough money for the fare – fled the famine by going abroad. Huge numbers took ship across the Irish Sea to Liverpool and many hundreds died there. Hundreds of thousands more went to other ports in Britain, or made the long and dangerous voyage to Canada, Australia and the United States. Wherever they went they took with them hunger, disease and despair. Many died of fever in the dreaded 'coffin ships', which carried human ballast across the Atlantic, or survived the voyage only to die in the quarantine stations and fever sheds of Quebec or Montreal. Almost a million famine emigrants eventually arrived in the United States, land of all their hopes, only to end their journey in the miserable slums of Boston or New York.

All these horrors were endured just two lifetimes ago, when Ireland was supposed to be part of the richest and most progressive country in the world – Great Britain. To this day, many Irish people, and many Irish-Americans, believe that the famine was not a natural disaster caused by the failure of the potato crop, but a deliberate act of genocide perpetrated by the British Government. So over the years the famine has become part of the legacy of bitterness surrounding British rule in Ireland, which Irish nationalists have always perceived as a long story of conquest and rebellion, of colonial rule, religious discrimination and injustice, which reaches back 1000 years and still jeopardizes the chances of lasting peace and reconciliation today.

In this sense, the famine was only one of the worst periods in 1000 years of political and economic oppression. In another, it was a watershed in history. The Roman Catholic Church gained an ascendancy in the years following the famine which it has not yet lost. Political developments at that time led to the rise of the Fenian organization, the Irish Republican Brotherhood (IRB), the movement towards a free and independent Ireland, and the rise of the Irish Republican Army (IRA).

Enormous social changes took place in Ireland itself. Many of the great landed estates were broken up and farming methods were transformed. The face of the land itself changed, with once populous hillsides and shorelines stripped bare of people, and neatly-squared fields replaced the intricacies of *clachan* and *rundale*, an ancient way of life. The last pre-modern society in Europe, with its complex social obligations and barter exchanges, was ousted by wage labour and

This sympathetic cartoon from The Lady's Newspaper *of 1849*
shows the Irish farmer beset with demands for rent and rates
while his young son points to America, the land of opportunity.

the cash economy. Irish traditions of music and dance, of poetry and story-telling, went into decline and the Irish language itself came close to extinction.

The Irish diaspora, that great migration across the face of the Earth, was given a massive impetus by the famine. The Irish immigrants, especially those to the United States of America, arrived full of anger and distress, then preserved those memories, like old photographs, to be handed on, only faintly blurred, to their children and grandchildren. Today, the President of the United States has to take those memories into account when he considers which way forty million people of Irish descent are going to vote, and the IRA knows where to look for money if political reconciliation fails to work out.

The memories of Irish people, like the folk memories of people everywhere, are an inextricable tangle of history and mythology, of slogans, songs and stories picked up on grandma's knee. Myth is painted in stark whites and blacks, images of good versus evil, and such stories are often more potent than history in shaping events. Unscrupulous leaders use them to sway the mob and motivate the terrorist. History is far more ambiguous. Motives are often mixed, bad actions are fired by good intentions, the villains turn out to have some redeeming features and their victims are not all saints or martyrs. So it is with the history of the Great Famine.

The difficulty is to try and put aside prejudice, to see events through other eyes than our own, and judge people's actions not by the standards of today, but by the standards of the mid-nineteenth century. If we succeed, there are ideas to be gained from the history of the famine which may prove more important than the passions inspired by mythology. They are ideas about the responsibilities of government and the duties of the rich towards the poor. As the one hundred and fiftieth anniversary of the famine passes, we can see that many people in Ireland itself have learned those lessons and have striven to apply them by helping people in countries less privileged than their own. In the end, this may be the single most important legacy of the famine, the realization that we all have a duty to help those weaker than ourselves. If we fail in that duty we may find that history will judge all of us as harshly as it does the British Government at the time of the Great Famine.

CHAPTER ONE

The COLONIZATION OF IRELAND

*W*ithout some grasp of Irish history it is very difficult to understand the famine. The underlying conditions which turned the failure of a single crop into a national disaster were themselves the product of the long and turbulent relationship between the Irish people and their English rulers.

The English did not conquer Ireland all at once, but in a long succession of invasions across the Irish Sea from the early Middle Ages onwards. Each invasion was followed by a period of settlement, when English barons and their followers were granted lands in Ireland. From time to time the Irish lords rebelled against the Crown and attacked the English strongholds. The descendants of some of the earliest settlers became so thoroughly assimilated into Irish life that they often ended up by joining the rebels. For centuries, the only territory securely in English hands was the rich farmland within the Pale, once a fenced enclosure, later a vaguely defined area to the north and west of Dublin. Beyond the Pale was Celtic Ireland, where the Irish people clung defiantly to their own ways. They kept to their own language, customs and elaborate social structure, with loyalties attaching to great lords in the four ancient kingdoms of Ulster, Leinster, Munster and Connacht.

The Irish never experienced the Roman conquest, nor the later encroachments of Jutes, Angles and Saxons from mainland Europe, but they welcomed

Illuminated figure of the Virgin and Child from the eighth-century Book of Kells. *Ireland preserved the Catholic faith through the chaos of the Dark Ages.*

St Patrick in the late fourth century and stayed loyal to the Catholic faith throughout the chaos of the Dark Ages, when the rest of Europe was plunged into pagan confusion. Along with most of the rest of Europe, the Irish suffered from Viking raids in the early Middle Ages and the Norsemen established important settlements at Dublin and elsewhere on the Irish coast. The Irish kingdoms were often at war with one another, but they combined forces against the Vikings and eventually succeeded in defeating them.

Following the Norman conquest in the late eleventh century, the Kings of England embarked on wars in Scotland, Wales and, above all, France, but throughout the Middle Ages the English were too preoccupied with other problems to ensure the complete subjugation of Ireland. Then, in the sixteenth century, England went through the traumatic experience of the Reformation and became a Protestant country and, in due course, most of Scotland and Wales followed suit. Ireland did not. The Irish people remained loyal to their own interpretation of the Catholic faith and stubbornly resisted all attempts at conversion.

During the sixteenth century, the whole of Europe was riven with sectarian warfare as Protestants struggled with Catholics for ascendancy. The two most powerful countries in Europe, France and Spain, emerged from the Counter-Reformation as strongly Catholic nations, politically and religiously opposed to England. The Tudor monarchs became increasingly uneasy at having a Catholic neighbour at their backs who might assist their enemies and made vigorous efforts to subdue the Irish lords. Elizabeth I eventually succeeded in establishing English control over almost all of Ireland and her name is still remembered with horror in many parts of the country. Some of her lieutenants, like the Earl of Essex, massacred large numbers of helpless people and conducted scorched-earth campaigns across great tracts of the land. These rebellions and brutal counter-measures culminated in an English victory at Kinsale in 1601. The two most powerful leaders, Hugh O'Neill and Rory O'Donnell, eventually fled the country in 1607 and, for a while, Irish resistance was brought to an end.

In an effort to insure against further upheavals, the English had already begun to confiscate large areas of land and settle them with 'plantations', colonies of English Protestants and Scots Presbyterians. After the battle of Kinsale they increased these efforts, especially in the most warlike province of Ulster. All over

Below: An engraving of Queen Elizabeth 1 dressed to kill. Her reign is still remembered with horror by the Irish.
Left: Robert Devereux, Earl of Essex. As the Queen's lieutenant he ordered massacres in Ireland.

VARIVS CROMWELL EXERCITVVM ANGLLÆ
ENENS ET CVBERNATOR HIBERNLÆ OXO

REIPVBLICÆ DVX GENERALIS. LOCVN
NIENSIS ACADEMLÆ CANCELLARIVS

Ireland they also seized the estates of defeated Irish lords and handed them over to English adventurers, known quaintly as 'undertakers', who were supposed to allocate lands to immigrant Protestant settlers. In practice there were rarely enough immigrants to go round and the new owners were often obliged to take on Catholic tenants from the local population. The net result was that Irish people, who had farmed the land for centuries, were either turned out of their homes and made to live on poorer land outside the Protestant enclaves, or forced to surrender their rights and live as tenants on estates they had once owned. Naturally, the Irish resented this ruthless colonization and continued to rebel whenever they saw that the English had other problems on their hands.

The internal discord in England which preceded the Civil War provided one such opportunity and the Irish rebelled on a large scale in 1641. They attacked the Protestant settlements, killing men, women and children without mercy. The Protestants eventually brought in troops from Scotland and responded with equal brutality, justifying the murder of Catholic children on the grounds that 'nits breed lice'. The Irish defeated the Scots near Armagh in 1646, and confused fighting ensued for three more years until Oliver Cromwell arrived to restore English rule in 1649. He laid siege to Drogheda and, when his forces eventually stormed the town, they massacred 3000 people, many of them innocent citizens who had taken no part in the battle. Cromwell sent a dispatch back to England:

> It hath pleased God to bless our endeavours at Drogheda … The enemy were about 3000 strong in the town. I do not think that 30 of the whole number escaped with their lives … I wish that all honest hearts may give the glory of this to God alone, to whom indeed the praise of this mercy belongs.

Cromwell combined religious bigotry with total ruthlessness. He slaughtered all those who opposed him. Those who did not were forced to leave their homes and take their followers across the Shannon, 'To Hell or to Connaught,' as he put it. The Great Protector then handed over most of the best estates in the

Oliver Cromwell: 'To Hell or to Connaught.'

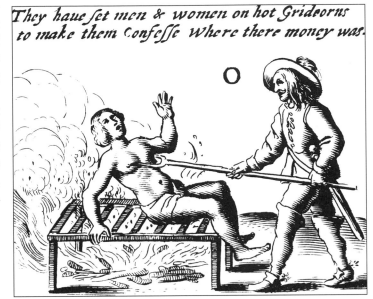

Right: Anti-Catholic propaganda in 1642. A pamphlet showing Catholics, in dashing Cavalier dress, torturing innocent Protestant women. Far right: Anti-Catholic propaganda during the 1798 rebellion. Irish Catholics with bestial expressions are once again murdering Protestant virgins.

They haue set men & women on hot Grideorns to make them Confesse Where there money was.

midland and eastern counties to his own followers and, by the time the blood had congealed, about eighty per cent of Irish land was in Protestant hands.

Forty years later, the succession of the Catholic king James II, his banishment and subsequent attempts to regain his throne, seemed to offer another chance of freedom to the Irish. The war which followed became rich in mythology, especially for northern Protestants, even though many of the troops who did the actual fighting were foreigners. The Jacobites succeeded in bringing in troops from France and Germany and laid siege to the walled town of Londonderry. The town's successful resistance is still celebrated by Ulster Protestants. William of Orange, the new Protestant king of England, now arrived on the scene together with his own army of European mercenaries. He also brought with him the blessing of the Pope, who feared that a Catholic victory would strengthen France too much for comfort. William then won a symbolically important victory at the Battle of the Boyne in 1690, which Ulster Loyalists also take care not to forget. When the war was over, the English tightened up their administration and for more than a hundred years Ireland was, sometimes uneasily, at peace.

About three-quarters of the Irish people remained doggedly Catholic, while their rulers made clumsy attempts to force the Reformation upon them. The

English established the Church of Ireland with its own Anglican priests and bishops throughout the land, and made the people pay tithes to support it. There were very few Irish converts. So, after the Jacobite rebellion, the Government tried to suppress Catholicism by force. Under a series of Penal Laws, dating from 1695, Catholics were denied freedom of worship. No Catholic could hold office or practise law. No Catholic could bear arms or serve as an officer in any of the armed forces of the Crown. Other laws were aimed at preventing Catholics from achieving wealth or social status. Catholics were forbidden to buy land and when they made their wills they were obliged to divide whatever land they owned between their male children. If one of those children chose to become a Protestant, he could lay claim to the whole of his father's estate. Catholics were also prohibited from serving an apprenticeship, from attending a school, and even from going abroad to study. The priests themselves were outlawed and threatened with branding or even castration.

In practice these laws were not always strictly enforced, but the effect was to oblige all Catholics to forsake their faith or resort to subterfuge. Some wealthy families elected to become Protestant, at least in name, in order to preserve their estates intact. Most people preferred to continue to practise their religion as inconspicuously as they could. Priests went into hiding and were sheltered by

The Battle of the Boyne, when William of Orange defeated the Jacobite resistance, is symbolically important to Irish Protestants.

members of their flock, sometimes at great risk to those providing the shelter. Mass was said in secret. In the countryside priests often held services at 'mass rocks' in isolated places, where soldiers or informers could be spotted at a distance. Catholic teachers taught children covertly at 'hedge schools'. The Penal Laws ensured a barrier of secrecy between a Protestant landlord and his Catholic tenants, encouraging deviousness on the one hand and distrust on the other. The Penal Laws were relaxed in 1782 and abolished altogether in 1829, but by that time it was too late. Any hope of Irish subjects becoming reconciled to English rule had been soured by religious discrimination and the Roman Catholic Church had become identified in the minds of many people with the oppressed Irish nation.

The Irish people were therefore, to a large extent, deprived of both religious freedom and economic opportunity, though they were not prevented from becoming merchants. The landed gentry would not stoop to trade themselves, but they recognized its importance as a means of augmenting their own wealth.

Throughout the eighteenth century, England treated Ireland as a colony, to be exploited in much the same way as other colonies in America, India, or elsewhere. Large sums in rent left Ireland every year to enrich English landlords living abroad. Raw materials, principally agricultural products, were exported to England in exchange for English manufactures carried in English ships. Restrictions were placed on Irish goods. The manufacture of woollen cloth was forbidden, as was the export of Irish glassware. English brewers even succeeded in blocking the export of hops, which meant that the Irish had to be satisfied with porter – or stout as it was later to be called – a taste which they have preserved to this day. These restrictions, some merely irritating, some commercially damaging, had the effect of retarding the development of modern trade and industry in Ireland.

Under English rule, the King's viceroy in Dublin, later known as the Lord Lieutenant, had enormous powers, but from the early seventeenth century onwards an Irish Parliament was called from time to time in Dublin. Of course Catholics could not serve as MPs until the Penal Laws were repealed, so Parliament was the preserve of the Protestant landlords and they were fiercely protective of their own interests. This did not always win them friends in England, where the upper classes tended to regard the Protestant gentry as rustic parvenus. Rejected by their peers in England, the Anglo-Irish also contrived to remain distant from their Irish tenants. They feared and despised the religion of the people and, for the most part, failed to understand either their culture or their language.

English was widely used in the eastern counties, but many people were bilingual and Irish remained common in the home. In remote areas it was often the only language until well into the nineteenth century. There were other, more subtle differences. Irish people had different priorities. Kinship obligations often extended well beyond the immediate family ties which the English understood. Where they were free to do so they often held land in common in a system known as *rundale,* which did not acknowledge individual ownership as a permanent state of affairs. Land holdings could be revised and reapportioned in ways which baffled English observers. In the far west, many communities remained semi-nomadic, travelling with their cattle to the mountain pastures in the summer and returning to winter quarters in the autumn. Such communities were deeply

conservative and highly resistant to change. To the English they seemed backward, recalcitrant, little better than savages.

Prior to the conquest, and in some areas long after it, the Irish had observed Brehon law, an antique legal system with its own hereditary lawyers. Unable to defeat their rulers in battle and unable to seek justice in courts which they did not understand and which were totally biased against them, Irishmen were obliged to find other means of redress. Already accustomed to secrecy in matters of religion, they readily took to other kinds of secret society. In the countryside they formed covert organizations such as the 'Molly Maguires', or 'Ribbonmen', so-called from their habit of disguising themselves in women's clothes. They might not

The impressive eighteenth-century architecture of Strokestown Park House, now the home of the Famine Museum. The Anglo-Irish landlords lived in the grand manner, but they had little control over the land.

be able to oppose the landlord by day, but by night they could maim his cattle or fire his ricks. If the occasion demanded it, they could even threaten his life. Throughout the eighteenth and early nineteenth centuries, agricultural 'outrages', ranging from rent strikes to arson, were a very effective means of restraining the powers of a landlord, though many attacks were also directed by one group of tenant farmers against another. In one county, Tipperary, 254 such incidents were recorded in a single year.

The Protestant ruling classes were therefore far more alienated from the people they governed than were the English gentry from English working people. They had gained the land by conquest in relatively recent memory and there was no community of interest between landlord and tenant, only a desire to maintain as much distance from each other as possible. This was reflected in the style in which many landlords lived, building large, pretentious houses to impress the natives with their dignity and power. The eighteenth-century architecture of Strokestown Park House in County Roscommon reflects this attitude at its zenith. There is a tunnel beneath the garden from the stable yard to the kitchen wing, at opposite extremities of the house, which protected the ladies and gentlemen within from the distressing sight of Irish servants passing to and fro. In the kitchen, there is a gallery from which the lady of the house could drop her menu for the day to the cook, without the unpleasant necessity of having to make personal contact.

In fact, many of these houses stood empty for large parts of the year. Anglo-Irish landlords often preferred to live in Dublin, or even in London, leaving the administration of their estates to local agents or middlemen. Whether absentee or not, the landlord was usually perceived as the monarch of his neighbourhood, with myriads of tenants obedient to his will. In reality, he usually sat at the top of a ramshackle pyramid of tenancies and sub-tenancies. Frequently, almost all the land on an estate would be rented out to tenants holding large tracts of land on long leases. The larger tenants, the so-called middlemen, then sub-let to small farmers. These smallholders were often 'tenants at will' – they had no security and could be thrown off the land at the end of the year – and the middleman would increase the rent year by year, a practice known as 'rack-renting'. The greater the number of smallholders, the larger the middleman's income, so it was in his interest to allow the land to be divided into as many holdings as possible.

This tendency was made worse by the practice known as sub-division. The Penal Laws on inheritance were repealed in 1782 and most large farmers, even if they were only leaseholders, handed on their leases to their eldest sons. Since these often ran for thirty-one years, sometimes much longer, the bigger farmers could often accumulate considerable wealth. Small farmers, on the other hand, had no means of providing for their children except by giving them a piece of land, and they continued to divide their holdings, often within their own lifetimes, between their sons and daughters. The result was that in many parts of the country the great estates were divided and sub-divided into ever-diminishing plots of land, but even these smallholders were not at the bottom of the heap. There was an even larger body of people who either had no land at all, or rented a tiny plot from one season to the next.

Many estates were also entailed. In other words, the nominal owner simply held it in trust for his descendants. He could not sell even a fraction of the land in order to invest the capital in improvements. On the contrary, he often took out additional mortgages, or 'encumbrances', in order to pay his debts or provide for his children. The result was that the landlord often had no interest in his estate except the rent from the middleman or leasehold farmers and he neither knew nor cared what happened to the thousands of smallholders who teemed on his estate. Even the larger tenants had no incentive to invest in the land, because there was no mechanism for compensating them for improvements and they might lose everything on the expiration of a lease. The whole system was a recipe for rural decay and neglect.

The availability of land was also limited by climate and geography. About a third of Ireland is mountain and bog. The soils in the mountains are too thin to support anything but rough grazing. Bog land needs draining before it can be cultivated and even then the soil is very low in nutrients and has to be heavily fertilized before it will grow good crops. In the west, the rainfall is too high for wheat. There is simply not enough sunshine for it to ripen reliably and before the advent of modern fungicides and grain-drying facilities it was not a worthwhile crop in many areas. Barley does better, and so do oats, but both required capital investment in drainage, or hand cultivation with the spade, which called for the employment of huge numbers of labourers. Neither of these options appealed to landlords with little direct interest in the profitability of the land. Instead, many of them spent their money on fine houses or dissipated their incomes on horses, gambling, and the pleasures of foreign travel.

Meanwhile, in eighteenth-century England, landlords were modernizing their estates, taking advantage of new systems of crop rotation, new methods of cultivation, new breeds of livestock. They were also busy enclosing common lands and turning smallholders off their estates. Some of these were taken on as agricultural labourers. Others moved to the towns, where the Industrial Revolution was bringing about even more radical changes. Unlike most of Ireland, England was becoming first and foremost an industrial country, where most poor people worked for wages. English capitalists were investing heavily in mining, railways, ports and industrial facilities, both at home and abroad.

Little of this investment flowed into Ireland, partly because there were few natural resources of coal and iron ore, partly because the Irish had a long and unhappy reputation for popular unrest. In the north east, from the mid-eighteenth century onwards, Presbyterian mill owners began to mechanize the linen industry, developing their own techniques for processing the cloth. Elsewhere, apart from the district around Dublin and a few areas in the south east, there was little industrial manufacture. Earlier restrictions on trade and the stifling effect of the Penal Laws had also retarded economic development. By the standards of the rest of the United Kingdom, Ireland was slow to develop a modern economy and slower still to develop an urban class of industrial entrepreneurs, who might have offered employment to a growing population.

The population of Ireland in 1791 has been estimated at between four and four and a half million. The census of 1841, which is generally reckoned to be an underestimate, gave a total of over eight million, which means that the population almost doubled in just fifty years. This was a higher rate of growth even than in England, where industrialization demanded an ever-increasing workforce, but growing numbers of town-dwellers in England meant a growing market for Irish corn. Although much of Ireland is better suited to the rearing of cattle, the eastern side of the country has more sunshine, a lower rainfall, and better soils. In these areas, from the late eighteenth century onwards, there was a shift from pasture to tillage as farmers took advantage of higher prices for wheat, oats and barley. Prices continued to rise when England went to war with France and they stayed high for more than a generation, until Napoleon was finally defeated in 1815.

This was a time of relative prosperity for Ireland's farmers, especially in the drier wheat lands in the south and east. Farmers renting twenty or more acres of land were able to do comparatively well and this period saw the gradual emergence of 'strong farmers' – Irish Catholic tenants, often holding long leases, who began to acquire some wealth and standing in the community. At the same time, as the Penal Laws were relaxed, a Catholic middle class of shopkeepers and professional people began to prosper in the towns. Irish towns and cities still bear witness to this period of prosperity, with long terraces and graceful squares of neat Georgian and Regency houses. Dublin itself developed into one of the most elegant cities in Europe.

Increasing prosperity was accompanied by increasing independence from England. The Anglo-Irish gentry raised a large force of volunteer militia to combat the dangers of a French invasion at the time of the American War of Independence. The English, with other preoccupations, raised no objections. While declaring their loyalty to the English Crown, Henry Grattan and his followers in the Irish Parliament succeeded in winning for themselves the power to push through their own measures without interference from London. It was not full-fledged independence by any means. The MPs were still mostly Protestants and most of them held great estates, which meant that the policies they advocated were far from revolutionary, but 'Grattan's Parliament' helped to provide many Irish people with a sense of national identity.

For some Irishmen this genteel dabbling in democracy was not enough. In the 1790s, fired by the ideals of the French Revolution, with its message of equality and universal brotherhood, groups of young patriots calling themselves United Irishmen began to agitate for full independence. Membership was drawn mostly from young, well-educated middle-class men, both Catholic and Protestant. Theobald Wolfe Tone, the most charismatic figure in the movement, was himself a Protestant and the organization was formed first in Belfast, where there was a very strong group of northern Presbyterian radicals. Like the Catholics, they too had suffered restrictions on their freedom of worship and had been denied access to office. Now, although the more conservative Presbyterians would have blenched at such a partnership, they joined with Catholic radicals in fierce demands for freedom.

The Government clamped down on the movement in 1794 and the United Irishmen looked to France for help. In 1796, Wolfe Tone persuaded the French to land a force of 15 000 men in Bantry Bay. In the end, storms divided the French fleet and the landing never took place. Nevertheless, the threat of a French invasion aroused all the ancient paranoia which the English and the Anglo-Irish felt about an alliance between Catholic rebels in Ireland and Catholic troops from abroad. The Dublin authorities called in the militia to root out the rebels. Raw undisciplined troops ravaged the countryside, brutalizing and torturing innocent

Hessian Dragoons in the Irish Rebellion of 1798.

Hessian Dragoons at the Battle of Vinegar Hill in 1798, when the United Irishmen were overwhelmed.

people, antagonizing many political moderates, who would not normally have opposed the Government.

Ironically, the formation of the United Irishmen took place at the same time as the emergence of a very different movement in Ulster. The Orange Order, commemorating Protestant victory at the Battle of the Boyne, developed as a sectarian movement among northern Presbyterians in Armagh. Many who had begun voicing their discontents by joining the United Irishmen switched over to the Orange Order in fear of a Catholic insurgency. When the rising eventually took place in 1798 it quickly took an ugly sectarian turn. The Ulster rebellion soon fizzled out, but Catholic rebels in Wexford massacred a large number of

Protestants and for a time seemed to pose a military threat to the Dublin administration. The British sent in reinforcements and the rebels were crushed at the battle of Vinegar Hill. Another French force made a successful landing at Killala, County Mayo, too late to be of any help to the main body of the rebels, and they too were forced to surrender. Protestant militias, many of them Orangemen, helped round up the Catholic insurgents. The cruelty with which they hanged, flogged and tortured people they believed to be sympathetic to the rebels only served to increase sectarian bitterness in many parts of the country.

The 1798 rebellion brought Ireland's flirtation with independence to an end. Britain proposed an Act of Union to make Ireland formally a part of the United Kingdom. The members of Grattan's parliament were persuaded, or in many cases bribed, to vote for the Union. The British Government also hinted heavily at full Catholic emancipation if the Irish bishops would lend their support to the Union. They did so, even though the last of the Penal Laws was not in fact repealed until nearly thirty years later. On 1 January 1801 the Act of Union became law, the Irish Parliament was abolished, and Ireland became part of Great Britain. In practice the Union was not wholeheartedly embraced, even by the English. Although there was a single currency, and, technically speaking, free trade between the two countries, the relationship continued to be very one-sided, with Ireland very much the poor relation. Nevertheless, it was a measure which was to have a profound effect on the management of all Irish affairs, including the administration of relief during the Great Famine. The Act of Union had one good effect as far as Ireland was concerned. It ensured that a hundred Irish Members of Parliament were granted seats at Westminster. At first they were, of course, mostly Protestants, but a few Catholics eventually succeeded in getting themselves elected. The most outstanding of these was Daniel O'Connell, a brilliant lawyer from Derrynane in County Kerry. O'Connell was a member of an ancient family and his uncle was a wealthy man who took an interest in his nephew's education. Daniel grew up in the west and learned Irish as a child, but he was sent to France to complete his education and he witnessed the turmoil of the French Revolution at first hand. The experience gave him a lasting distaste for violence, which was to influence his own political career.

In Parliament, O'Connell used his lawyer's skills in debate and he was a clever politician, who was able to influence events more than the size of his following would suggest, by making an adroit succession of alliances with the Whigs in the House of Commons. He was also an outstanding public orator, able to appeal to huge crowds of ordinary people even more successfully than he could sway a courtroom. He campaigned first for full Catholic emancipation, which was finally achieved in 1829. Then he set out to win repeal of the Act of Union. This was a limited aim. O'Connell always maintained his loyalty to the English Crown, but he wanted self government for Ireland, and an Irish parliament with the power to legislate on Irish affairs.

The Repeal Movement was vigorously resisted by the Protestant landlords, who saw it as damaging to their own interests. It was also opposed by many English MPs who saw it as the beginning of the slippery slope which would lead ultimately to an independent Ireland. O'Connell, therefore, relied increasingly on huge public meetings to generate demands for repeal. He calculated, wrongly as it turned out, that these would in themselves frighten the British authorities into agreeing with his demands. In 1843, almost on the eve of the Great Famine, his supporters organized a vast rally at Clontarf, just outside Dublin. The meeting was banned by the Government. Some of the more hawkish Repealers urged O'Connell to ignore the ban, march on Dublin, and force the issue by sheer weight of numbers, but the authorities were fully prepared and had artillery trained on the meeting ground. O'Connell shrank from bloodshed and the suffering he knew it would entail. He ordered his followers to disperse and the monster meeting came to nothing. For the moment, the movement for Irish independence was stalled.

These great events may not have had any immediate bearing on the lives of ordinary people, unless they happened to attend one of O'Connell's mass rallies. The increased prosperity of the farmers earlier in the century may also have meant very little to poor people as they struggled to make a living. But at least while wheat prices were high the farmers were ready to take on labourers, especially at harvest time, and even part-time labour was better than none. Up to about 1830, many poor people were also able to take advantage of a boom in the linen trade. The manufacture of linen from flax was not highly developed in England and there was a flourishing export trade across the Irish Sea. The wet Irish climate was well suited to the cultivation of flax and an extensive cottage industry developed in many different parts of the country, with poor people able to supplement their incomes by growing and preparing flax and spinning it into yarn for the weavers.

Unfortunately for Ireland, this minor boom in cottage industry and agriculture did not last. When the Napoleonic wars came to an end the price of grain and other agricultural products fell. Prices for all forms of produce seem to have reached their nadir around 1831 and then picked up slightly, but they did not recover the heights of 1815. The cottage industry in linen also declined as factory production increased. The development of mechanical spinning and weaving benefited only one area, the counties of Down, Antrim and Armagh in the north, where Protestants were still in the majority. In fact, the growth of the mechanized linen industry may have been one reason for the expansion of the Orange Order, as Presbyterian linen workers sought to prevent Catholics from sharing in the trade. By the 1830s, towns like Belfast and Lisburn in the north had already entered the industrial age, while the rest of Ireland was still overwhelmingly dependent on agriculture, and farming was again in difficulty.

While the price of grain had been high, so had rents. When the grain price fell, rents also declined, but not enough to help those at the bottom of the heap. During the prosperous times the population had grown in proportion to the resources available to feed it. Now, although the actual rate of population increase began to decline, there were very large numbers of people competing for relatively small areas of available land, so those with small plots to rent, principally the larger tenants, were in a sellers' market. This meant that the poorest members of the community – up to a third of the total population – had to give up growing grain for their own consumption and turn instead to potatoes, because potatoes were the only crop which could support a large family on a very small acreage. This dependence on one crop, not just for prosperity, but for very survival, was to have fearful implications for the poor people of Ireland at the time of the Great Famine.

CHAPTER TWO

The POTATO CULTURE

*T*raditionally, Ireland had been almost entirely a pastoral country. Both the climate and the customs of the people were well adapted to the keeping of cattle, but an increasing population meant that people had to turn more and more to the cultivation of the land. The only crops which will flourish even in the wettest districts, always remembering the need for drainage, fertilizer and intensive cultivation, are potatoes. No one knows exactly when or how they were introduced into Ireland, except that it was almost certainly not by Sir Walter Raleigh. Whenever it was, potatoes do not seem to have come into widespread use until the eighteenth century, but by the end of the century they had become the staple food of the poor. For the most part, poor people grew their own crop for their own consumption. Potatoes are very bulky and expensive to transport and they will not keep from one season to the next. Except in those districts where there was a large nearby town they were not readily saleable, so the smallholders had very little connection with the cash economy and lived from hand to mouth, from one season to the next.

Potatoes are highly nutritious. If you eat enough of them you get sufficient carbohydrate and protein to supply your body with almost everything it needs. The only serious deficiency is in fats and vitamin A and they were usually supplied, even in the poorest of families, by a little buttermilk – the residue left

Girls earthing up potato ridges in County Antrim. These were the so-called 'lazy beds', an ingenious form of cultivation which English observers failed to understand.

behind when cream has been processed for butter. A working man in those days would eat up to 14 lb (6.5 kg) of potatoes a day – a prodigious quantity for a modern man even to think about, but it kept him in good health. Irish recruits in the army were, on average, slightly taller than their fellows in England, and proportionately robust and well made. Irish women were also healthy and highly fertile, so families were frequently large.

Arthur Young, an Englishman who toured Ireland in the late 1770s, reported that an acre of manured land in Mayo would yield up to 12 tons of potatoes. A man, his wife and four children consumed about 5 tons a year, the produce of less than half an acre. Assuming a holding of an acre, this left them with a surplus to feed a pig, a few chickens, and to keep a cow or two through the winter. To supply anything like the same nutritional value from cereals would have required at least three times as much land and far greater amounts of labour.

In the first half of the nineteenth century, the people with the greatest dependence on potatoes were landless labourers or cottiers, living in one-roomed cabins which they built for themselves or with the help of neighbours out of stone and turf. Most of the poorest people survived by trading their labour in exchange for a plot on which to grow their own food. As the population increased the plots grew smaller and smaller until cottiers were far worse off than those whom Arthur Young had observed in Mayo. By the mid-1840s some men were having to keep their families on as little as a quarter of an acre. A cottier would live and work on such a plot by agreement with a farmer, usually a tenant farmer, who might hold a lease for twenty or thirty acres. The cottier would then work for the farmer at a notional rate of wages – say eight pence a day for 120 days – especially at seed time and harvest. In return he would get his patch of ground, where he would build his own cabin and spend his spare time cultivating his potatoes.

Alternatively, a landless labourer might build his hovel on a piece of waste land and rent a plot of land as conacre, a yearly lease of ground on which to grow potatoes. The soil was often manured in advance by the farmer and would be reclaimed by him as soon as the potatoes were harvested. Conacre was often preferred by the poor, because the rent did not fall due until the crop was ready in November. It was disliked by many farmers for precisely the same reason. If the crop failed, the farmer would not get his rent. Conacre rents were frequent in Connacht, while the cottier system was more common in Munster and Leinster.

Although neither system gave the poor any security, access to land was probably easier in Ireland than in most parts of Europe and the fact that a young couple could set up their home and support themselves on a tiny plot of potatoes was one important reason for the dramatic increase in population.

These arrangements suited the farmers very well. Either they got cheap labour or they got high rents. Land for which the farmer himself might be paying thirty shillings (£1.50) an acre, could be sub-let for four to five pounds, in some cases even ten pounds, an acre. For the most part these poor people paid rent not in cash, but in kind. The landlord put his own valuation on a day's labour, or on a pig or a crop of grain, and took that in lieu of actual money. Those labourers who depended on a cash income in addition to the potato crop could rarely earn more than five or six pounds a year*. The poor man at the bottom of the heap, he who could least afford it, paid the most in rent. Contrary to popular belief, rents were not nearly as high as they were in England, but wages were also far lower and poverty far more widespread.

Growing potatoes was a complex and highly sophisticated business. The system of cultivation in general use called for the construction of ridges, known as 'lazy beds' to prejudiced observers. The technique varied in detail from one part of the country to another, but the basic principles were always the same. Instead of breaking the ground and digging deep, as an English gardener might do, the Irish cottier cut parallel lines through the turf, some three or four feet apart, and piled the space between the lines with lime and manure which he had collected throughout the year. Close to the sea, he would also make use of sea sand, with its admixture of lime-rich shells, and seaweed, especially the heavy kelp from the low-water line.

---

*To make sense of nineteenth-century prices you first have to convert them into modern denominations and then measure them in terms of purchasing power. The pound sterling was the standard unit and the English and Irish currencies were of equal value, just as they are today. There were twelve pence to the shilling, and twenty shillings, or two-hundred and forty pence, to the pound. In mathematical terms, a nineteenth-century penny was equivalent to less than half a modern penny, a shilling to five modern pence and so on. But then you have to allow for inflation. An acre of arable land in Ireland will fetch £250-300 in rent today, as against anything between one pound ten shillings and ten pounds then. A large loaf of bread which now costs about 75p would have sold at that time for 2½ pence (twopence halfpenny). A stone (14 lb) of potatoes, on the other hand, which might easily cost £2 today, would only have realized threepence or fourpence in the nineteenth century, except at times of great scarcity. Broadly speaking, money was worth fifty to a hundred times what it is today, but labour was extremely cheap and the living conditions of poor people were closer to those of modern Africa than to those of modern Ireland.

Beginning at the outer edge, he then sliced underneath the turf and turned it over, grass-side down, so that there was a kind of fertilizer sandwich between two layers of turf. He would turn both sides towards the middle to form the ridge, with shallow trenches on either side. With a small sharp tool called a spud, he would make holes at regular intervals through the upturned sods of turf and plant the seed potatoes into the filling of the sandwich. He finished the ridge by piling on earth from the trenches on either side, thereby raising the whole bed a foot or more above the surrounding soil. This method gave excellent drainage on wet soils and ensured that the seed potatoes came into direct contact both with the manure and the fertile interface between the two layers of turf. It was an extremely laborious and highly ingenious form of horticulture, thoroughly understood and practised by Irish men and women for centuries, which English observers usually failed utterly to comprehend.

Modern archaeologists have now demonstrated that ridges of this kind had been used in Ireland to grow grain for at least 5000 years. The nineteenth-century cottiers also grew some oats and barley on ridges which had grown a crop of potatoes the previous season. In some districts, if they could afford it, people kept back some oats or barley for their own consumption. Potatoes are an excellent food, but they are very difficult to store. Leave them in the ground and they are liable to rot. Lift them in the autumn, line a pit or a clamp with straw, and cover them with a thick layer of earth and they will keep until the spring, but by May, or June at the latest, most of them will be no longer fit to eat. There is then a long hungry gap from early summer until the new crop is ready in the autumn, and this period was often known as the 'meal months', because oat or barley meal had to be consumed to stave off a period of starvation.

Since there was no way he could hold over a supply of food from one season to the next, as a grain farmer would do, the Irish cottier had nothing to fall back on in a lean year. The only way he could store the food value of his potatoes was to feed them to livestock. Almost all cottiers kept a pig, but almost always this would be taken in lieu of money for the rent. Meat of any kind was a great luxury for the Irish poor. Even their potatoes were often of poor quality.

Quick-maturing varieties, such as the so-called 'new' potatoes of today, did not yield enough to repay the labour of growing them. During periods of relative prosperity there was a whole range of different kinds, such as 'cups', 'apples', or 'pinkeyes', but during the nineteenth century the poor relied increasingly on a variety known as 'lumpers', a coarse and high-yielding potato which required less fertilizer. It was very late maturing and would keep well, but even lumpers would not last much beyond May. So poor Irish people were always in want during the summer and were obliged to try and supplement their food supply in any way they could.

In Mayo, Roscommon and Donegal it was quite common for a labourer to plant his potatoes on his conacre plot in the spring and then leave home to seek work on farms on the other side of the Irish Sea, leaving his family behind. Often, his wife and children were obliged to take to the road and beg their way through the summer months until the potato harvest came round again. The sight of poor families begging shocked many wealthy visitors to rural Ireland. Some regarded them with compassion. Others saw in this chronic distress evidence of a fecklessness which they took to be characteristic of poor Irish people, who were looked on as being too stupid and too lazy to look after themselves.

It is true that the poor people in many parts of Ireland were often very close to starvation even in relatively normal times. The problem was that this wonder food, the potato, which had permitted the vast increase in population, was subject to the risk of frost damage in a hard winter and always liable to infection. In a good year poor families could get by well enough, even though their living conditions were primitive. They had enough to eat and enough surplus for their livestock. They could keep a cow or a few goats on rough grazing and use the excess potatoes to feed their pigs and chickens. They could also cut enough turf to keep them warm through the winter. If they lived close to the sea they had access to fish, shellfish, and a plentiful supply of seaweed fertilizer for the potato beds. But everything depended on the success of the crop. If the potatoes failed, they were in trouble and, at least from the early nineteenth century onwards, such disasters were all too common. There were fourteen complete or partial crop failures in different parts of Ireland between 1816 and 1842, and, as a result, there were severe food shortages in parts of the country.

Many observers were aware of this. Joseph Sabine, Secretary to the Horticultural Society in London, writing in 1822, noted the virtues of the potato as a highly nourishing food and regarded its increasing use with alarm: 'the extension of the population will be as unbounded as the production of food, which is

A late nineteenth-century farmer, with horse and slide car, outside a farmhouse in Ulster. Only the rich would have owned a wheel cart.

capable of being produced in very small space and with great facility.' He then pointed out that potatoes were vulnerable to 'casualties of the season' and made a dire prediction: 'a general failure of the year's crop, whenever it shall become the chief or sole support of a country, must inevitably lead to all the misery of famine, more dreadful in proportion to the numbers exposed to its ravages.'

The Third Earl of Rosse, a conscientious resident landlord in Kings County (now County Offaly), carried out many improvements on his estate, digging land drains, installing modern machinery, and encouraged his tenants to do the same by offering them financial compensation. He also forbade any further sub-division of land and recommended emigration for young people. Reflecting on these changes in 1843 he believed he had averted a dreadful calamity: 'the population continuing to increase, till, in ordinary years, it was but barely fed, a year of scarcity would at length come, and with it a visitation of the most awful famine, such as the history of the world affords many examples of, a famine followed by pestilence.'

The Duke of Wellington made a similar observation in 1838. So if there were many who were aware of possible catastrophe, why did they do so little to avert it? The first thing to bear in mind is that the potato crop had never failed for two years running. By tightening their belts and with some help from the authorities, the poor had always been able to survive previous failures. The fundamental problem, in any case, was the lack of alternative forms of employment, aggravated by the land tenure system. Many saw that there was a need for land reform in Ireland, but they shrank from the implications. The rights of property were held in very high regard by the propertied classes and land reform smelt too much of revolution and the guillotine. Governments also had a much more limited view of their responsibilities than they have today. Charles Trevelyan, the civil servant who was to have such a vital, one might say fatal, role in the administration of famine relief, put it like this:

> The proper business of a Government is to enable private individuals of every rank and walk of life, to carry on their several occupations with freedom and safety, and not itself to undertake the business of the landowner, merchant, moneylender, or any other function of the social life.

*A farmhouse with potato ridges in Connemara. This building
is far more substantial than the hovels of the poor people who were
the most frequent victims of the famine.*

What the Government did do was to hold a Poor Enquiry in 1835, which, taken together with the census in 1841, revealed the full extent of Irish poverty. Almost half of all farms in Ireland were of less than five acres. Two-fifths of the population were found to be living in 'fourth-class' accommodation – one-room cabins built of mud, turf or loose stone, lacking a chimney or proper windows, and almost invariably damp and unfurnished. Smoke from the fire escaped through the leaky roof and the occupants often slept on piles of straw on the bare earth, usually sharing this accommodation with the family pig and chickens, if they had any. Although middle-class observers probably underestimated the amount of time spent in cultivating potatoes, cutting turf and looking after the livestock, neither men nor women were in anything like full employment. Such poor people would probably not have survived, certainly not in such large numbers, anywhere else in rural Europe. They owed their high fertility, their large families and their relative health to the mildness of the climate, the availability of turf for fuel and the abundance of the potato crop. But even by the standards of the time it was a wretched existence. Everyone agreed something had to be done about the Irish poor, but it must be done without upsetting powerful vested interests.

One solution was to modernize agriculture and there was some progress in this direction during the first half of the nineteenth century, but it was difficult to achieve without first clearing the land of large numbers of small tenants who would have no other means of making a living. This led many people to advocate emigration to the colonies. In fact, up to half a million Irish people had already left the country, but throughout the eighteenth and early nineteenth centuries, the great majority of those willing to undertake the long and hazardous journey across the Atlantic were Protestants from the north. Presbyterians of Scottish descent were well aware that their own ancestors had moved from one country to another and they also knew that both the United States and the Anglophone provinces of British North America were countries where dissenters like themselves had taken refuge and prospered in previous generations. In Nova Scotia and New Brunswick there were also many Scottish immigrants, creating the kind of society where Ulster Protestants would feel at home. In the United States there were frontier lands where able and energetic farmers could buy land at low prices and make their own way. The 'Ulster Custom', whereby a tenant could sell his tenancy when he decided to move, gave these emigrants enough money to start a new life.

Natives of the Catholic south and west of Ireland felt very differently, especially in the Gaelic-speaking areas. Here, people lived in close communities, linked by close kinship ties, and could often trace their attachment to a particular piece of land through many generations. No matter that the legal ownership might be vested in some distant landlord and that the land might have been divided and sub-divided many times; the ancestral ties remained. People saw access to land as the means of preserving life. Those who could rent a big enough patch to grow sufficient potatoes to see them through the year, and who could scrape together the rent from one half-year to the next, survived. Those who could not joined the army of itinerant beggars who were always the first to starve when times were hard. There was nothing to be gained from surrendering a tenancy, only a loss of well-tilled land and a cabin which may have been poor enough, but was better than nothing. People with any claim to a plot of earth, however tenuous, clung to it with desperation. They were rooted in the land of Ireland and they did not give up those roots easily.

Although it was some time before the effects were felt in the more remote communities, things began to change in the early years of the nineteenth century. During the Napoleonic wars, English merchants found it more difficult to reach traditional timber supplies in the Baltic and turned instead to British North America. Here, good-quality timber was cheap and plentiful. Millions of logs were felled and floated on rivers down to the Atlantic seaboard. In primitive shipyards in towns like Saint John and Chatham, New Brunswick, shipwrights put together crude, but capacious ships to carry the timber across the Atlantic. They called these slab-sided vessels 'coffin' ships because they were thrown together and notoriously liable to sink.

The transatlantic timber trade grew and flourished, but it had a built-in disadvantage. The traffic was all one way; ships returning from England to the timber ports had to sail under ballast, their holds loaded with stones or gravel to keep them on an even keel. Some shipping agent had a bright idea. The Atlantic colonies were crying out for more people to open up the wilderness and meet the growing demand for labour. Why not fill the holds with poor emigrants looking for a new life on the other side of the Atlantic? Just fit wooden bunks down either side of the main hold and the rest would be easy. The human ballast would walk on board and save the trouble and expense of loading stones. The voyage out to Canada would then be even more profitable than the journey back and everyone would be happy.

There was another, more sinister precedent to the emigrant trade. Liverpool, like Bristol, had grown fat on the slave trade. Ships would put out for West Africa, load up with slaves and carry them to the West Indies. Having sold their slaves they returned to England with holds full of sugar, but since Britain had banned the slave trade in 1807, many of the companies once engaged in it had gone through a lean time. The answer to their problems lay in carrying fare-paying passengers instead of slaves. Conditions on board would be much the same, with one or two significant differences, as we shall see in Chapter Five.

Shipping agents started to tout for trade throughout Ireland and gradually the number of Catholic emigrants increased, aided by the agricultural depression which followed the ending of the Napoleonic wars. By the mid-1840s the trade in passengers was already more profitable than the trade in timber and 68 000 emigrants, a large proportion of them Catholics, made the perilous journey in 1844. Before the famine, and still to some extent after the worst years were over, the departure of a family, or even a single individual, for North America was traumatic for the whole community. Everyone knew that it was extremely unlikely that emigrants would ever return. Their departure was a kind of death, and like a death it was celebrated with a wake.

People would gather from miles around for an 'American wake'. There would be a pipe of tobacco and a glass of *poitin* for each guest, music, dancing, and farewell speeches, and when the time came for the emigrants' departure, the wailing and weeping was as deeply felt as if they had died.

So although increasing numbers of Irish Catholics were beginning to emigrate, there was still a good deal of resistance to the idea among ordinary people. In the higher flights of society, some people like Lord Rosse were in favour, but many, including some powerful voices in the Catholic Church, were opposed to it. In the late 1830s, emigration had still not made much impression on the legions of the poor. At the same time, there was increasing pressure on the Government to do something. Instead of addressing the root of the problem and reforming the land tenure system, it proposed an elaborate cosmetic exercise, which it hoped would take the beggars off the street and so remove them from the public mind.

The result was the Poor Law Act of 1838, very much modelled along the same lines as a similar act in England. Even at the time, there were many critics of the new legislation who maintained that it was utterly inappropriate to Ireland's real needs. The Government went ahead with it anyway. Under the Act, Ireland was divided into 130 areas, known as unions because they were formed by joining together several parishes, and a workhouse was erected in each union. The work-house was administered by a Master and a Matron, under the supervision of a Board of Guardians, elected by the ratepayers of the district. All costs were to be met from local rates levied on local landowners and tenants.

The first generation of workhouses were built to a standard pattern, devised by an English architect, and all 130 of them were run up in the years between 1841 and 1845. They were austere, but rather imposing buildings, built so solidly from stone that many of them have survived for 150 years and are now converted into local hospitals. The reception area at the front housed administrative offices and washrooms, where new arrivals were stripped of their old clothes, forced to wash and issued with a workhouse uniform. Behind this was the main block, with projecting wings at each extremity. This building had dormitories for men on the right and women on the left and workrooms on the ground floor. Behind this was

Bird's-eye view of a workhouse, showing the reception building at the front, the main accommodation block in the middle and the infirmary at the rear.

the kitchen and eating hall and chapels for the different denominations. Behind this again was an infirmary, consisting of smaller rooms for the aged and the sick. The whole extraordinary complex was surrounded by a high stone wall and the enclosure was sub-divided by further walls into separate yards for men, women, boys and girls.

On entering the workhouse the members of a family would immediately be separated, deprived of their own clothing, deprived of their identity. Husbands were divided from wives, children from parents, brothers from sisters. Any attempt to meet, except during Sunday chapel, was severely punished, sometimes by a flogging, sometimes by solitary confinement in a lock-up. Existence inside these grim institutions was totally regimented, the hours and activities marked by the tolling of a bell. Men were put to work breaking stone, women to sewing or domestic activities, children to rudimentary schooling. The diet was barely sufficient and the accommodation was spartan. The whole workhouse philosophy was punitive and the atmosphere as chilling and humiliating as possible. The Government wanted to keep paupers out of sight, but it did not want them to enjoy the experience.

The English were always apt to think of the Irish poor as incorrigibly lazy, though in fact their reluctance to work had more to do with a lack of incentives than incapacity for hard work. A man tied to a contract of labour in exchange for land at a very disadvantageous rate would have been a fool to sweat too hard, especially if he had to dig his own patch when his work for the farmer was finished. Once removed from the constraints of life in Ireland, the Irish often showed themselves to be prodigiously hard-working, which is one reason why they were so much in demand as labourers, or 'navvies', in England itself. But the prejudice was still there, so under the Irish Poor Law there was no possibility of outdoor relief – no arrangement by which the poor could get a free meal, even though this existed in England, where the poor were considered to be more industrious. The only relief available in Ireland was inside the workhouses and people could only gain admission by demonstrating, under intensive questioning, that they had no other means of support.

Once inside, a family was only permitted to leave as a family. Men or women were not allowed to go off by themselves to try and make better arrangements for their children. It was feared, not unfortunately always without reason, that some parents might be tempted to dump the children and never come back for them. The Government was almost paranoid about the prospect of allowing a dependent class of paupers to live off the state, so the operation was deliberately limited in scale. Workhouses came in different sizes, according to the size of the local community, but they were never intended to house more than about one per cent of the population at any one time. Taken together, they could only provide accommodation for about 100 000 people. As intended, the poor people hated them and avoided entering them at almost any cost. Until the Great Famine came, the workhouses were three-quarters empty.

Having said all this, it would appear that the Poor Law was just another instrument of oppression inflicted on the poor Irish people. From a modern point of view it may well seem so, but there was also an element of philanthropy and it is possible to see in the Poor Law the first faint glimmerings of the idea of the welfare state. At least the workhouses were meant to prevent the utterly destitute from starving to death and Victorian philanthropists saw it as their moral duty to inculcate the virtues of hard work, discipline and sobriety. We also tend to forget that some of the most distressing aspects of the inmates' lives, such as the separation of men from women and parents from children, are still a feature of many modern hospitals. In the end, perhaps the worst thing about workhouses was that they represented the failure of a family to provide for itself.

However poor they were, Irish people would have feared that sense of shame, and some of them were very poor indeed. Along the western seaboard, where soils were very acid, rainfall very high and land very cheap, there were huge areas where landlords or their agents were very thin on the ground, but the numbers of poor people scrabbling for a living along the shoreline were very high. Such districts, in western Mayo and Galway, or parts of Donegal, were just too remote and infertile to be of much interest – at least for the time being – to rapacious landlords, and the people were too poor to be worth exploiting. Since the only crops which could be grown with much success were potatoes, which were unsaleable in such remote districts, the people who survived there were sub-sistence farmers. They lived only off what they could grow for themselves and survived almost entirely outside the cash economy.

They were not there by accident. There was a rich harvest of wrack to be won from the sea, which made the important task of fertilizing the potato beds comparatively simple. They also had access to sea sand, with its admixture of lime-rich shells. Modern archaeologists have shown a continuity of occupation in these areas running back for 5000 years and ancestors of the nineteenth-century families may well have been there for centuries. The potato culture, however, had created and sustained a hugely increased population, all trying to live in the same way, in the same places, and according to the same customs as their ancestors had lived before them. It was a life rich in tradition, in story and music, but it was, at the best of times, an extremely precarious existence.

In 1838, Lord George Hill, a younger son of a wealthy family in County Down, bought up a number of small properties in Gweedore, an isolated area of Donegal. The district was remote, but not unlike many similar areas in western parts of Mayo or Galway. The local people, all Irish-speaking and still deep in their ancestral way of life, were wretchedly poor. They lived in *clachans,* tiny clustered villages with one-roomed houses jumbled together close to the shore, and held their lands in accordance with the old *rundale* system, which meant that a man might have the use of a dozen or more tiny patches of land, unfenced and scattered higgledy-piggledy over the cultivated ground. In the summer, the younger people would migrate with their cattle to summer pastures high in the mountains, a custom known as *boulay.* These ancient customs had survived unchanged for centuries, but shortly before Hill's arrival, the local schoolmaster, Patrick McKye, sent a letter describing the desperate state of the people to the Lord Lieutenant in Dublin.

He began by recording his own journeys in Ireland, Canada and the United States, then observed that in all his travels he had 'never witnessed the tenth part of such hunger, hardships and nakedness'. The 9000 or so inhabitants of the parish had only one cart, one plough and thirty-two rakes between them, all other agricultural work being done with the spade. Although their homes were surrounded by huge areas of untilled land, their farms were 'so small that from four to ten farms can be harrowed in a day with one rake'. The people shared their unfurnished houses with their cows and the dung was cleaned out only once a year. Many of the children went naked and hundreds wore 'filthy rags, most disgusting to look at', but the reason for McKye's distress was that the whole community was threatened with starvation because of a 'rot or failure of seed in the last year's crop'. Many families, he said, could afford only one meal every two

Interior of a cottage in western Ireland, 1890. Fifty years after the famine, the houses of the poor still had little furniture, earthen floors and no chimney for the fire.

days, 'their children crying and fainting with hunger, and their parents weeping, being full of grief, hunger, debility and dejection, with gloomy aspect, looking at their children likely to expire in the jaws of starvation'.

The previous landlords had been absentees and the agents negligent. Some tenants were up to ten years in arrears with their rent and many had never appeared on any rent roll. Given the conditions in which the people lived this was hardly surprising, but Lord George Hill was determined on change. He was full of good intentions, but his arrogance was breathtaking. He had absolutely no doubts as to the value of his own ideas and the worthlessness of ancient Irish tradition. He simply assumed that he knew better than the local people how they should live their lives, and, like the enlightened colonial benefactor that he took himself to be, he set about dragging them into the nineteenth century.

The first thing he perceived was that the problem was not a shortage of land – there were thousands of acres stretching in all directions – but a shortage of drains. The people could work the sandy soils immediately behind the shoreline, but the bog land further inland was too wet to cultivate with the tools at their disposal. They also lacked the seed with which to grow new crops and a market in which to sell them. So Hill built a quay, which would allow trading ships to put into the harbour, and set up a store stocked with everything from awl blades to wheelbarrows, which he was prepared to sell at very little over cost. Since the people did not have any money, the store bought hides, butter and oats for cash. Previously, almost all the grain in the parish had gone for the distillation of *poitin,* or illegal whiskey. Lord Hill soon put a stop to that. The store bought nearly four-hundred pounds' worth of grain in its first year of business and did a brisk trade in almost everything but alcohol. He also instituted the business of buying knitted woollens from the women, putting a little money into their own pockets and starting a trade which would later flourish all over the west.

Hill then set about re-allocating the land. First, he gave his tenants notice to quit for non-payment of rent, explaining that they would have new and larger holdings when he had finished his reorganization. He had taken the trouble to learn Irish before he started, so they understood the meaning of his words even if they did not agree with his plans for their welfare. He explained that the land would be divided into neat rectangles, 'long cuts', from foreshore to hillside, each firmly fenced with stone. The old *clachans* would be broken up, and each tenant would then have to build a new house on his own strip of land. He would be shown how to dig drains and how to maintain them. Great care would be taken to ensure that no one received less land, or inferior land, to the holding he had farmed before. On the contrary, he would have far more.

The only thing the people would have to surrender were the mountain pastures where they had grazed their cattle. Hill himself had plans to reserve the mountains as grazing for his own sheep. He assured his tenants that, with scientific drainage, their own cattle would have better grass in the fenced fields. He may have been right, but to Hill's surprise, his call for volunteers to fence the new fields went unanswered. When he hired a man to build walls, the people pulled them down by night. They did not like the idea of abandoning their *clachans* and living in houses separated by fields and stone walls. Lord George noted with surprise that 'the pleasure the people feel in assembling and chatting together made them feel the removal of the houses … a great grievance'. The people may also have disliked the idea of abandoning the hill pastures where they had grazed their cattle for thousands of years, where they had gone every summer to the *boulay* villages in the mountains. They may even have disliked the idea of never being able to drink *poitin* again. It is possible that they foresaw, with some clarity, the ending of an entire way of life, a culture which was far older than Lord George Hill's and from their point of view far richer in music, poetry, and everything else that makes life worth living.

Eventually, Hill bribed and bullied his tenants into doing most of what he wanted. He offered annual prizes for the cleanest cottage, fattest pig, best vegetable patch, best woolly jumper. He built a Protestant church and tried to push his tenants into that, but here they resisted him. In all other things they reluctantly complied. He made them fence their lands, drain them, and diversify their crops so that they could market some of them and forego their dependence on potatoes. He then put up the rents and made sure that everyone paid them. Since the rise was from £472 to a total of £1100 from more than 700 paying tenants, and their incomes had greatly increased, it was not beyond their capacity to pay. The community prospered and so did he. His work was much admired by other improving landlords and by distant sponsors in London, and heartily disliked by most of his tenants. He had forced them out of their own ways and into the unpoetic world of the cash economy, and they did not love him for it.

Hill was the archetype of the do-gooding colonizer, who always knew what was best for the natives and was not averse to making a profit out of it. His writings are full of a smug superiority, which must have been difficult for his tenants to stomach, but when the Great Famine came, Lord George Hill and some of the other 'improving' landlords in the neighbourhood paid for imports of meal out of their own pockets and were very active in organizing relief. Hill himself relentlessly lobbied the authorities for more food supplies, and insisted, in flat contravention of Government policy, on selling it for less than the price charged by local dealers. There was hunger and considerable suffering, but very few people died. In fact, the numbers of people in the Dunfanaghy union, where Hill was Chairman of the Board of Guardians, actually increased during the famine. On less well-managed estates, and there were very many of them, and along the great swathes of coastline from Connemara to Malin Head, where the people still lived in the old ancestral ways, men, women and children were to die in their thousands and their hundreds of thousands, and an ancient way of life would die with them.

CHAPTER THREE

The HUNGER

One morning early in September 1845 the director of the Botanic Gardens in Dublin noticed that the leaves of some of the potato plants in the trial plots were going black and curling at the edges. He duly reported what he had found and, on 6 September, a short account of an outbreak of the new potato disease appeared in the Dublin *Evening Post*. Within a week there were reports of similar outbreaks in a number of different places and the authorities knew they had a grave problem on their hands.

The fungal infection we now know as Blight, *Phytophthora infestans*, had already made its appearance earlier in the year in England and on the Continent. In fact it had devastated the potato crop in the Eastern United States for the past two seasons. In Ireland, with so many people dependent on the success of the harvest, failure of the potato crop was a matter for alarm. The losses in 1816, 1822 and 1831 had been so severe that they had required Government intervention, but in these and other failures the problem had usually been local and it had never affected the whole crop. Dry rot affected some plots, or some varieties, and not others. Early frosts hit some parts of the country and left others untouched.

The first essential was to find out how widespread the infection really was, so the Government ordered the constabulary all over Ireland to inspect the crops in its own districts and report back. Many of the reports were reassuring. In

A contemporary print of a starving mother and children begging for food during the famine.

Dunfanaghy and around Letterkenny in Donegal the effects appeared to be very light. In Monaghan about half the crop was rotten. In Valentia, County Kerry, a correspondent reported that the people were eating the sound parts of the diseased potatoes and feeding the rest to their livestock. In her diary, Elizabeth Smith, the wife of a County Wicklow farmer, noted:

> The potato failure has been much exaggerated, the disease is by no means as far spread as was supposed and the crop so over abundant that the partial failure will be the less felt, particularly as the corn harvest was excellent. But people were much frightened and this caused a run on the Savings Bank which might have encreased the evil, that too is luckily over, so the prospects for winter are brightening.

This of course was in a very prosperous district, but even in the worst-hit areas the infection seemed to affect some fields – those, for instance, on low-lying clay lands – and left others in the peat bogs or on the hill tops unscathed, though appearances were often deceptive. Blight is a capricious disease. If it strikes early in the season, the foliage withers and turns black and the tubers never have a chance to develop. If it strikes late, as in parts of Ireland in 1845, some early varieties will escape altogether. With the main crop, the potatoes appear to be sound when they are lifted, but the tubers rapidly develop black bruise-like marks beneath the skin and are reduced eventually to a black, squelchy, stinking mess. The poor depended on the late maturing 'lumper' and their crops were particularly liable to this vile corruption.

By October, potatoes were found to be rotting in widely scattered areas of Ireland, particularly in Waterford, Antrim, Clare and Monaghan. In these districts, and in many parts of the west, poor people were soon in distress. The Government set up a scientific commission to try and find out the cause of the new disease and to recommend ways of preventing its occurrence. The commission was hampered by the limited scientific knowledge of the time and failed even to recognize that Blight was a fungus infection. The scientists came up with a number of useless methods for preventing the rot and some even more dubious ideas for making the best use of potatoes which had already been infected. Their most practical suggestion was a laborious method for reducing

A contemporary illustration of the effects of potato blight. The causes of the disease were not recognized at the time and no effective remedy was found until many years after the famine.

grated potato to starch, but they admitted that starch in itself has hardly any nutritional value and recommended mixing it with oat or barley meal in order to make it go further.

There was a need for more immediate action. A Relief Commission was set up in Dublin, with local relief committees all over Ireland. These were empowered to buy food for distribution to the poor, to be paid for out of private charity and small public donations. In London, the Tory Prime Minister, Sir Robert Peel, was so alarmed at the prospect of food riots that he introduced a coercion bill to maintain public order. There were loud objections and he was unable to get it passed by the Commons. In a more humane move, Peel also ordered a supply of Indian corn, the grain we now know as maize, without even telling his own cabinet. In order to maintain secrecy, he placed the order with American shippers through a firm of private bankers and set up a commissariat organization to control its distribution.

Peel's aim was not to give corn away free, but to sell it at just over cost price, and so set up a hedge against a rise in food prices. If commercial dealers knew that the Government had an unknown quantity of corn, which it might release on to the market at any moment, they would take care not to allow prices to rise too high for fear of being undercut. However, the scheme would not work if the dealers knew just how little grain there was in the Government stores. Security was maintained and the trick worked. Peel spent about £140 000 on two shipments of Indian corn, which would have lasted only a few weeks if it had been released all at once. Sold in small quantities at one penny a pound, the small supply of Government corn helped to avert disaster.

The meal was popularly known as 'Peel's Brimstone', because its bright yellow colour reminded people of sulphur. At first it was greeted with some suspicion. Although it had been used in famine relief before, maize was not a familiar grain in most parts of Ireland. In some cases, parish priests had to show people how to prepare it and also eat it themselves before anyone else would touch it. Peel's choice of Indian corn was deliberate. Not only was it the cheapest food available, but there was no pre-existing domestic market in maize. The sanctity of the market was very much a part of British political thinking. Any Government interference, unless it was thought to be for the benefit of the

Right: Sir Robert Peel, the Tory Prime Minister in 1845-6. His secret purchase of Indian corn helped stave off Irish hunger for the first year of the potato blight. Inset: Daniel O'Connell, whose huge rallies demanding the repeal of the Act of Union alarmed Peel and his government.

country as a whole, was regarded with deep suspicion. Even as it was, many Irish merchants complained noisily about Peel's interference with their profits. This resentment was to influence Government policy the following year, but for the moment Peel's secret store answered its purpose.

The Government knew that poor people had very little money with which to buy food at any price, and it turned to a traditional method of famine relief which had worked successfully in the past. It invited local committees in distressed areas to make bids, presentments as they were called, for public works. What the authorities had in mind were new roads, quays, landing stages, and other improvements in public amenities. The Government would contribute half the cost as a long-term loan and the rest would have to come out of the local rates. In those areas with active local committees there was a rush to get as much public money as possible and the Board of Works in Dublin was almost overwhelmed with applications.

Since Ireland was a part of the United Kingdom, all these measures for famine relief came under the control of the Treasury in London. The Assistant Secretary at the Treasury, and the civil servant effectively in control of all famine relief, was Charles Trevelyan. Trevelyan was an able man, a devout Christian, conscientious and hard-working, but he had a number of failings which were to have unhappy consequences for the Irish poor. He had a profound belief in the rightness of his own opinions and often rejected advice from people far better informed than himself. He only made one short visit to Ireland during the period that he was in charge of relief and even then he never went beyond Dublin. He also found it extremely difficult to delegate, constantly insisting that far-off officials in remote districts should bypass their own channels of communication and write direct to him. Despite his immense capacity for work, this inevitably meant that some matters needing an urgent decision were delayed longer than necessary. These failings might not have mattered if he had not also been blinkered by some of the fashionable prejudices of the day. One was an almost superstitious belief in the rectitude of free trade, placing God and Mammon firmly in the same camp. Another, as we have already seen, was a strictly limited view of the responsibilities of Government.

During the emergency of 1845–6 Trevelyan's powers were not exercised to their fullest extent. He did not get on well with Sir Robert Peel and he had not yet won the degree of autonomy he was later to acquire, but he kept a very sharp eye on public spending. The Public Works were fairly effective in providing employment, especially in Clare, where the need was great and the local committees were active, but these were subject to a number of abuses. Committee members would sometimes ensure that their own cronies got work, while far more needy men went unemployed. Often the works themselves were pointless. There were complaints that perfectly good roads were being dug up and re-metalled to no apparent purpose. Sometimes the pay clerk failed to turn up on the appointed day, or arrived without enough money, and the men and their families had to go hungry.

In other areas, where there were no works and no convenient relief centres, there were many cases of distress, but few people died from actual starvation. The worst effect of the first year of the famine was that many families disposed of their small assets to see them through the lean times. They sold their live-stock, pawned their clothes or their fishing tackle, got into arrears with the rent and into debt with the local meal merchant. The village money-lender, known as the gombeen man, often charged extortionate rates of interest. People who borrowed money to buy food had no means of repaying the debt. They had survived one year of hardship. They could not survive a second.

In July 1846, Peel's government fell. Peel had been in difficulty for some months and had actually resigned the previous year, only to be called back to form a government when the Whig opposition failed to do so. For some time past he had been determined on the reform of the Corn Laws. These laws were the relic of an earlier, strongly protectionist political philosophy, imposing tariffs on imported grain in order to keep home-produced grain prices high. Irish farmers benefited from similar policies, especially during the war years, when there was an immediate need to encourage domestic production.

Now the war was long over and the Industrial Revolution was in overdrive; the cities of England were full of workers demanding cheap food and their employers, anxious to keep wages low, backed up their demands. Overseas producers, especially in the United States, were able and willing to undercut the artificially inflated prices on the domestic market. Peel saw the logic of the argument. His Tory supporters, landlords and farmers almost to a man, were dead against it. Peel carried the bill reducing tariffs on imported corn, but only with Whig support. On the next bill before the House he was defeated, mainly through the defection of his own disgruntled supporters.

The effect of these events on Ireland was disastrous. The expectation that wheat prices would fall (though in fact they did not fall very much) meant that farmers in grain-growing areas were even less willing to take on labour, so the poor suffered an even greater level of unemployment. The other, greater misfortune was that the new Whig administration was dedicated to free-market principles. The Whigs believed, with almost religious fervour, that the best way to ensure prosperity for any country was to reduce government interference as far as possible, and to remove all restrictions on free trade. As a matter of convenience, they managed to reconcile this belief with some anomalies, such as the legislation confining trade with British ports to British ships, but the basic belief in free trade was unassailable.

Lord John Russell, the new Prime Minister, was a rather austere man, not lacking in compassion, but convinced of the truth of this doctrine. His Chancellor, Sir Charles Wood, had even more robust views and seems to have regarded Irish distress with some impatience. A degree of rather supercilious prejudice against the Irish was common on both sides of the House. Memories of 1798 and the much more recent disturbances surrounding O'Connell's demands for repeal of the Act of Union were still fresh in the minds of English politicians. They felt that the Irish were constantly holding out their hats for help, while rejecting John Bull's generous desire to teach them the joys of English sovereignty. Political cartoons of the period show this very clearly.

That summer, the potato plants looked healthy and all the signs pointed to a plentiful crop, but within a month of the change of administration in London, disaster had overtaken Ireland. In a celebrated letter, the great apostle of the Catholic temperance movement, Father Mathew, recorded his impressions:

On the 27th of last month, I passed from Cork to Dublin, and this doomed plant bloomed in all the luxuriance of an abundant harvest. Returning on the 3rd instant [August], I beheld with sorrow one wide waste of putrefying vegetation. In many places the wretched people were seated on the fences of their decaying gardens, wringing their hands and wailing bitterly the destruction that had left them foodless.

Captain Mann, a naval officer stationed in County Clare, which had already been hard hit the previous year, made similar observations:

> The first alarm was in the latter part of July, when the potatoes showed symptoms of the previous year's disease; but I shall never forget the change in one week in August. On the first occasion, on an official visit of inspection, I had passed over thirty-two miles thickly studded with potato fields in full bloom. The next time the face of the whole country had changed; the stalk remained bright green, but the leaves were all scorched black. It was the work of a night. Distress and fear were pictured on every countenance and there was a great rush to dig and sell, or consume the crop by feeding pigs and cattle, fearing in a short time they would prove unfit for any use.

After months of privation during the meal months of summer, the poor were already famished. Now many were staring at death. In the Killary harbour on the borders of Mayo and Galway, one of those coastal districts where people swarmed along the shoreline, there were reports of starvation as early as August. By September, appeals for supplies of meal were pouring in from commissariat officers and relief committees all over the country. The Government stores, still with some supplies left from the previous year, remained closed.

Sir James Dombrain, Inspector-General of the Coastguard Service, had the audacity to permit the free issue of meal in several distressed districts in the far west. As soon as he heard about this unauthorized act of charity, Trevelyan issued a public rebuke. Dombrain's proper course was to form a committee of local dignitaries, persuade them to make voluntary donations, which might be later augmented by Government funds. Trevelyan was ignorant of conditions on the west coast, but Dombrain knew them from first-hand experience. 'There was no one within many miles who could have contributed one shilling ... The people were actually dying,' he wrote. Trevelyan refused to believe it. He did not realize that landlords in these remote areas were almost all absentees and that people lived almost entirely without money from one generation to the next. Trevelyan also refused to believe that the distress was really acute. In his view 'the scramble for our own supplies is indicative, not so much of a general destitution, as of a perfectly natural desire to get food where it can be had at the cheapest rate'. Trevelyan was convinced that the relieving officers on the spot lacked his own acuteness and were easily deceived by cunning Irish farmers into parting with precious Government supplies for which there was no real need.

Many British officials, even some of those on the spot, also failed to understand why many poor farmers did not consume the oats or barley which they had grown, but the people did not dare. They needed the grain to pay the rent. If they did not part with the grain they would be evicted, famine or no famine, and if they lost their land they knew they had no hope. Of course, there were probably farmers here and there who were out to make a little money on their own account and saw Government hand-outs as an easy option, but they were in no way representative of the hordes of impoverished people who now besieged the Government grain stores. As the weeks passed, and some of the appeals from his own officials grew more and more insistent, Trevelyan reluctantly authorized the release of small quantities, but the truth was that the stores were almost empty and he could see no immediate way of refilling them.

As early as August, he had tried to persuade Baring Brothers, the bankers he had used the previous year, to buy a small supply of grain. Barings referred him to a firm of corn merchants who reported that supplies were almost unobtainable. By one of those historical ironies which make bad situations worse, the whole of Europe had suffered a poor harvest. Prices were high everywhere. The governments of France and Belgium did not scruple to interfere in the market place and bought up large quantities of grain for distribution to their own starving peoples. Many people in Ireland, including some highly respectable Tory landlords, called upon the British Government to do the same, but Trevelyan, supported by the Chancellor, Sir Charles Wood, persisted in his policy of non-intervention. He believed that private enterprise would swiftly fill the gap, importing and distributing supplies of grain far more effectively than the Government, regardless of the fact that over large tracts of Ireland there were no corn merchants who had ever attempted such an enterprise. What they could and did do was to buy Irish grain for export to England.

On the eastern side of Ireland there was a considerable surplus and the better-off farmers were happy to sell it as usual for the English market. Poor people were often outraged to see food leaving their own districts when so many

Left: Lord John Russell, the Whig Prime Minister at the time of the famine. He was not unsympathetic, but was profoundly ignorant of conditions in rural Ireland.

Below: Sir Charles Trevelyan, Assistant Secretary at the Treasury, the civil servant in charge of all famine relief.

Bottom: Sir Charles Wood, Chancellor of the Exchequer in Russell's government and responsible for keeping relief to a minimum.

were in need. In market towns throughout the country there were protests during the winter of 1846 and the spring of 1847 against the movement of food from one district to another. Even cartloads of Indian corn on their way to the Government depots were under threat. Mobs of people held up the carts and divided the contents among themselves. At some ports there were serious riots when it became apparent that shipments of grain, bacon, butter, or other food-stuffs were destined for export to England. The Government's response was not to stop exports, but to continue the shipments under armed guard.

There were also calls for a prohibition on distillation and brewing. Between them, brewers of Irish porter and distillers of whiskey consumed enormous quantities of grain, even at the height of the famine. The high consumption of alcohol was recognized as a problem in Ireland at the time and many temper-ance reformers, like the indefatigable Father Mathew, tirelessly campaigned to reduce it. Again the Government refused to intervene on the grounds that to do so would have been to interfere with free trade.

Blight had completely destroyed the mainstay of the diet for half the population. Putting a stop to brewing and diverting small quantities of butter and bacon would not have made any real difference, but it would have demon-strated that the Government was willing to compromise its own principles in order to save lives. In that case it would also have had to extend the ban on exports to shipments of wheat and other cereals to England and suffer a short-fall in domestic supplies. And this it flatly refused to do. There was no question, in Trevelyan's view, of inflicting shortages on the English as well. This percep-tion, when it became widely known in Ireland, made a nonsense of the idea of equal partnership between one part of the United Kingdom and another. Some parts, particularly the English parts, were more equal than others.

For the British Government to change its policy at that point would have taken an act of political will, and a readiness to spend vast amounts of public money, which was unthinkable to the politicians and civil servants concerned. In the first place there was a constitutional difficulty: the Government would have had to admit that sending grain from Ireland to England, which was, as we have seen, a long-established trade, was really exporting it rather than merely sending it from one part of the United Kingdom to another. Then there were enormous practical problems. There were at least three million Irish people in need, the great majority in the west, where food was at its most scarce. If the Government had stopped exports, prohibited brewing, bought up all the available grain and other foodstuffs at market prices and found some means of distributing it to the people in the areas where it was most needed, it might have fed at least some of the famished hordes for a few weeks and grain prices would never have reached the heights they were to achieve that winter. Some lives would still have been lost, but many might have been saved and the Government would have shown that it cared about the fate of the Irish people.

In fact, the Government preferred to stick to a political principle, and save money, rather than respond to the generous impulse to feed as many people as possible, no matter what the cost. What made it worse was that there was always some food available for those with the money to pay for it. The market at Skibbereen was said to be full of produce on more than one occasion during the height of the famine, while people starved to death within sight of it.

Trevelyan addressed the issue of prohibiting exports when he came to write *The Irish Crisis.* He believed that interference with the market would have caused even greater problems, because it would have deterred Irish grain traders from risking their capital by importing maize. In fact the merchants had already given notice that they would not take the risk if the Government repeated Peel's intervention of the year before. In the event, the traders went ahead and placed their orders and, contrary to popular belief, imports of grain into Ireland greatly exceeded exports from the beginning of 1847 onwards. If merchants had been denied their profits, those orders might never have been placed and cheap grain might never have reached Ireland at all. In the long run Trevelyan may well have been right. The problem was that it took time for traders to organize the shipments and time for the maize to cross the Atlantic. And time is one of the many commodities which starving people do not possess.

As before, the Government had decided on Public Works as the main method of relieving distress. Public Works as a form of famine relief were flawed in more ways than one. Hard physical labour demanded a high-calorie diet, which was precisely what the famished labourers lacked. Work on new roads, or rebuilding old ones, was no more productive now than it had been in 1845. If major works were to be carried out, the real need was for large-scale drainage schemes to bring more of the vast stretches of unproductive bog into cultivation, but the Government was opposed to most of these on the grounds that drainage schemes would benefit some landlords and not others. The same principle was at work here: no matter how great the need, or how good the objective, there must be no Government interference in the private sector. Ironically, the Public Works were already in flat contradiction to that principle because they removed large sections of the labour force from agriculture at a time when work on the land was of more importance than ever before.

The new Labour Rate Act recognized none of these problems, but it differed from its predecessors in several respects. Convinced that many people had been shirking on previous occasions, Trevelyan recommended that the new act should avoid paying a flat rate to each man. Instead, labourers should be paid for piece work – so much money for so much weight in broken stone or so many yards of road dug up. The formulae for assessing these rates were to be worked out by engineers and surveyors on the spot. In fact there were nothing like enough suitably qualified officials to inspect the work, especially in remote areas. The provision was, in any case, a recipe for unfair discrimination, for corruption and delay, and was eventually discarded as unworkable. The biggest problem of all, however, was that the money available for a day's labour was no longer sufficient to buy enough food to keep a man and his family alive.

A fit man could earn about a shilling a day on the roads, but few could make more than 8d, and in the winter of 1846–7 Trevelyan's market forces were working inexorably against the poor. With no brakes on speculation, those few traders who had secured supplies of meal could charge what they liked for it and prices rose accordingly, until corn meal was selling for three shillings a stone, or 3d a pound in small parcels – three times the price it had reached under Peel's administration. Two or three pounds of corn meal per day divided between a family of four or five, sometimes more, did not provide enough nourishment to keep its members alive for long. Eventually the family would die, and in the meantime they suffered from a vile clutch of deficiency diseases.

Scurvy was common as corn meal, unlike potatoes, contains no vitamin C. In advanced cases the sufferers' gums swelled, their teeth fell out, their limbs were covered in black sores, and death often followed from gangrene. Small children also suffered from protein deficiency, which could result in marasmus, the dreadful premature ageing which turns little children into wrinkled gnomes

Men and women on 'Public Works' in western Ireland in the
1890s. Periodic famines continued in remote areas until the late
nineteenth century and the same methods were used for relief.

with hair all over their faces. Some people, especially the elderly, were also
afflicted with famine oedema, the accumulation of fluid in the lymphatic system,
which makes limbs swell up like sausages. The horrors of this condition were
described by a visiting American, Elihu Burritt, who saw men working on the
roads with their limbs 'swollen to almost twice their usual size', and a boy whose
distended body had 'burst the ragged garment which covered him'.

Everyone eating too little food over too long a period would also have been
affected by acute anaemia, which reduces sufferers to complete exhaustion and
greatly lowers resistance to disease. This doubtless explained why so many were
said to be 'idling' on the works. The men were often robbing themselves of
nourishment in order to feed their children, and still trying to perform heavy
manual work on the roads. They were working on a negative balance of calories
and hastening their own deaths from starvation. The result in some cases was
heart failure. They dropped dead with a shovel in their hands.

Asenath Nicholson, an American woman who was travelling in Ireland at the time of the famine, recorded a bleak description of the effects of the gradual withdrawal of food:

> … a person will live for months, and pass through different stages, and life will struggle on to maintain her lawful hold if occasional scanty supplies are given, till the walking skeleton becomes in a state of inanity – he sees you not, he heeds you not, neither does he beg. The first stage is somewhat clamorous – will not easily be put off; the next is patient, passive stupidity; and the last is idiocy.

A more agonized impression came from Captain Wynne, a British officer working on relief in County Clare. When an overseer was attacked by 'Molly Maguires' near the small town of Clare Abbey, Wynne was ordered to suspend the Public Works in the district until the assailants had been brought to justice. He complied with the order, but he wrote to the authorities, pointing out the effects of this mass punishment on the ordinary people:

> … although a man not easily moved, I confess myself unmanned by the extent and intensity of the suffering I witnessed, more especially amongst the women and little children, crowds of whom were to be seen scattered over the turnip fields, like a flock of famishing crows, devouring the raw turnips, mothers half naked, shivering in the snow and sleet, uttering exclamations of despair whilst their children were screaming with hunger; I am a match for anything else I may meet with here, but this I cannot stand …

The Public Works in Clare Abbey were resumed, although the assailants were never arrested. In fact, considering the dreadful plight of the people, there were remarkably few acts of violence in Ireland during that long deadly winter and when they did occur they often had the ring of just retribution about them. The *Irish Free Press* reported a story about a murder at Kilcoran, County Tipperary.

> It appears that a man named Thomas Mulcahy, who had the reputation of an usurer in the country, was on his way from the sessions

at Cashel, where he had obtained several decrees against people indebted to him, when he was waylaid and barbarously murdered, his throat being cut, his head dreadfully fractured, and a large stone pressed upon his breast … The scene of the murder was within two hundred yards of the police barracks.

Apart from occasional killings, there were widespread attacks on food convoys and food stores, but these seldom involved bloodshed, because the mobs were very large and determined, while the defenders of Government property were not willing to risk their own lives for a principle. Usually they retired from the scene and went to fetch the police. By the time the police arrived, the food had disappeared. Confrontations between mobs of angry people and the authorities often dissipated at the moment when violence looked inevitable. When the Public Works were threatened with closure at Caheragh, near Skibbereen, 1000 men took their spades and marched into the town. Their way was blocked by a squad of soldiers with levelled muskets. The local magistrate called upon them to disperse and many of the men called back that they would 'as soon be shot as not'. But when they were given a small handout of biscuits and a promise that the works would not be halted, they quietly drifted away.

The same sentiment about a quick death being better than slow starvation was echoed by another Cork man in a curious story reported in the *Illustrated London News.* Three men, on the run after committing a murder near Bantry, were taken in and given food and shelter by people sympathetic to their case. On 12 December 1846, one of the three men surrendered to the police. He said that he could no longer take food from the friends who were protecting him because they were starving themselves. He was soon followed by one of his companions and the last of the three gave himself up on Christmas Eve. This man, one W. Downing, 'had been an athletic man, but his frame was so shattered and his countenance so haggard, that he was not recognized until he gave his name. He said that he supposed he would be hung, but even that was preferable to the horrid death which awaited him if he remained at large any longer'.

Hardly surprisingly, thefts of cattle, sheep, and of course turnips, were widespread. A Cork magistrate in the autumn of 1846 was continuously engaged in hearing cases brought by farmers against poor people caught stealing turnips. When the magistrates themselves pleaded for compassion the farmers protested. Some of them took the law into their own hands and shot turnip thieves on sight. Cattle and sheep were often killed and butchered in the field, making it impossible to identify where the meat had come from, but any poor man found with meat would certainly have been arrested on suspicion of theft. Conviction for cattle stealing almost invariably resulted in a sentence of transportation, usually to Australia. Before the famine there were about 600 such sentences in Ireland every year, but by 1847 the number had risen to 2000. No doubt, for many, transportation was preferable to starvation.

In their desperation many people tried to eat anything they could get their hands on. Before the onset of winter they turned to the famine foods which had always been familiar – common weeds such as sorrel, nettles, charlock, all of which are a useful source of vitamins, but very low in calories. On the coast they gathered shellfish and edible seaweeds such as dulse and carragheen. When these became scarce they turned to the coarser growths, like the various kinds of wrack which piled on to the beaches during the winter storms. Trying to eat these resulted in vomiting and diarrhoea. Fishing was out of the question for almost everyone. The weather that winter was described as 'one continuous

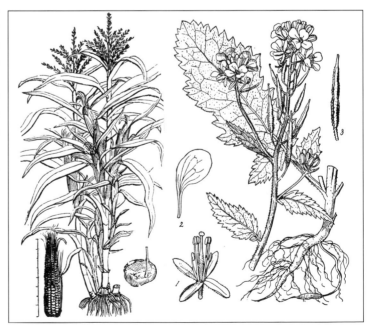

Right: Maize, then known as Indian corn. Imports of maize helped to relieve the famine throughout Ireland.
Far right: Charlock, one of the common weeds which were gathered by the poor when there was nothing else to eat.

storm'. The curragh, the frail native fishing boat, demands great strength and stamina to handle, even in a flat calm. There were very few jetties or wharfs along the west coast and in the fearful weather of 1847 most of the under-nourished fishermen could not even row beyond the breakers on the shore. Four fishermen who did go out in Belmullet, County Mayo, were drowned while attempting to rescue their nets. Another four perished in similar circumstances in Kilkee, County Clare, and there may well have been many more such cases in other parts of the country. Most fishermen pawned their nets and bought what food they could.

In many towns, inquests were held on people who starved to death during the early winter. In several cases the jury returned verdicts which implied neglect by the Board of Works and in one famous instance the jury found the dead man a victim of wilful murder by Lord John Russell and his colleagues. But as the fearful winter dragged on, the courts were overwhelmed and inquests were forgotten. Sextons were no longer able to keep up with the number of burials and there was a drastic shortage of coffins. In several towns they came up with the solution of a coffin with a hinged base, which could be opened to let the dead body slide into the grave, so that the coffin could be reused. Funerals ceased to be attended by mourners and women no longer keened as they followed the corpse to burial. Great trenches were opened up in many church-yards and the bodies were dumped inside, covered with quicklime. For a people who had placed such emphasis on the ceremonies surrounding death, this dreadful lack of ceremony filled people with a sense of despair which stayed with them, long after the worst of the famine was over.

A painfully simple statement of an ordinary man's feeling about this was recorded by a reporter for the *Limerick and Clare Examiner* late in 1848. Near the town of Kilkee, the visitor noticed a stretch of arable land, which had been left uncultivated because of a shortage of seed, and he stopped to ask a bystander why the land had not been tilled. The man replied:

> It wasn't tilling we were thinking of, but the hunger – we had nothing to put in it. When the famine came, they died, as the birds do when the frost comes, and [we saw] what we thought we would never see, they were buried without the coffin.

CHAPTER FOUR

SOUP AND SOUPERS

*A*s the famine deepened and the shortcomings of Government relief measures became more apparent, many people did what they could to relieve the hunger of the poor. There was a particularly generous response from people in the United States. Asenath Nicholson was an American Protestant evangelist, whose mission was to distribute bibles to Irish Catholics, but she quickly set about feeding as many people as she could, regardless of their denomination. She used her own money until that was exhausted and then distributed supplies sent by friends in the United States.

Almost all distributors of famine relief, whether private individuals or large charities, soon discovered that it was a mistake to hand out uncooked food. All too often it would be taken by the recipient, often the man of the family, and sold off round the corner in exchange for liquor or tobacco. The best way of ensuring that food reached the people who needed it most, especially the children, was to serve cooked food. So the usual system was to set up a soup kitchen, boiling up meal and vegetables in huge cauldrons and serving it out to ticket holders – people known to be in severe distress who would come to the kitchen every day.

Soup kitchens were nothing new. Private charities had run these institutions for many years in the slums of London and Dublin. Alexis Soyer, the

Soup kitchen during the famine, with charitable visitors looking on. Soup kitchens were first organized by private charities and were later operated on a vast scale by the Government.

famous chef at the Reform Club in London, devised a notorious recipe, which he claimed to be both nutritious and palatable. It went like this:

¼ lb leg of beef, 2 oz dripping,
2 onions and other vegetables as available,
½ lb flour (seconds), ½ lb pearl barley, 3 oz salt,
½ oz brown sugar, 2 gallons water

Melt the fat in a large saucepan and stir in the flour with sufficient water to make a roux. Add the remaining ingredients. Raise to boiling point and simmer gently for two hours, stirring occasionally.

Compared to some of the soups which were served up at the time of the famine this recipe was relatively luxurious. Most kitchens eventually settled on 'stirabout' – a kind of porridge made from corn meal, rice or oatmeal, according to what was available. The addition of meat, even in minute quantities, was the exception rather than the rule, but wherever possible the soup was supplemented with a bread or biscuit ration which provided some solid nourishment. The object was to feed as many people as cheaply and quickly as possible, and soup saved many lives during the famine.

Even some landlords established soup kitchens. The Marquess of Waterford wrote to his agents in different parts of the country, instructing them to feed the poor, and provided them with a rather more generous recipe than M. Soyer's. The Marquess of Sligo shared the cost of importing a shipload of meal with his friend, Sir Robert Gore-Booth, set up huge boilers on the terrace of his house, and set about shooting all the game for miles around to make soup for the poor. But the most important charities involved in the distribution of food were the British Association, to which Queen Victoria subscribed two thousand pounds, and the Society of Friends.

The Friends, usually known as Quakers, were a tiny community with only a few hundred members in Ireland, but many of them were prosperous business people, well organized and efficient. They made contact with other Quakers in Britain and America, arranged imports of grain and set up a distribution network, usually making use of Church of Ireland rectors to act as local agents.

In most cases, the supplies sent by the Quakers were also distributed in the form of soup.

Sadly, there was a small minority of evangelical clergymen who had already acquired a reputation as 'soupers', pressing people to convert to Protestantism in exchange for food. 'Taking the soup' therefore acquired an evil reputation among Catholics, and many people are said to have preferred to starve rather than accept the poisoned chalice offered by Protestant churchmen. To be fair, souperism was not a straight trade-off along the lines of 'first sign the Thirty Nine articles, now here's a bowl of soup'. It was more subtle than that. Slightly more subtle.

Some years before the Great Famine, there was an evangelical movement in the Church of Ireland which mirrored similar developments in Britain. A group of clergymen mounted what they were pleased to call 'The Second Reformation' and established 'missions' along the west coast of Ireland, where they judged the people to be in need of support, both materially and spiritually. The missions provided some local employment, erecting buildings and developing farms, and often gave practical help to the community, especially by introducing new farming methods and medical clinics, but their chief purpose was to save souls. Having created a degree of economic dependency in the local people, the evangelicals set about seducing them away from the Church of Rome. The programme of instruction usually included bible classes for adults and a school for their children. The children would be given a free meal along with lessons and the curriculum, of course, included a large dose of religious instruction. The chief principle of souperism was to get them young.

One of its most successful exponents was the Reverend Edward Nangle, the son of an army captain from County Meath. Nangle first came to the west coast on board a ship carrying meal to relieve the starving inhabitants of Achill Island, off the coast of Mayo, during the localized famine of 1831. He quickly discovered that the people were extremely poor, even in the best of years, and that there was only one priest ministering to several thousand people over a very large area. As soon as he got the chance, he set about raising money from sympathetic evangelical organizations in England, Ireland, even in the United States. Having obtained the support of his bishop and the lease of some land on the island, he returned to Achill and began to build his 'colony'. He was energetic. He had learned Irish, could preach in the language, and was a skilful fund raiser. The mission grew and prospered.

By March 1847 he had established a model farm, several schools, a hospital, a dispensary, a hotel for his many visitors, and a printing office for his newspaper, the *Achill Missionary Herald*. He had made hundreds of converts, by his own account, though whether the conversion was more than a temporary arrangement was another matter. He had also attempted, though without much success, to extend his missionary activities on Clare Island to the south and to the area of Ballicroy on the mainland to the north east. He was providing

*Fishermen with their curraghs on Achill Island c.1885.
These light boats take great strength and agility to handle and
undernourished fishermen were unable to use them during
the famine.*

Left: The Reverend Edward Nangle, a Protestant evangelist who preached against Catholicism during the famine.

Below: Nangle's 'colony' on Achill Island was viewed with intense hostility by the Roman Catholic clergy, resulting in a conflict for souls, when the real priority should have been feeding the people.

paid employment to over 2000 people, about a third of whom made no pretence of being anything other than Catholics. He had also imported a shipload of meal and was feeding more than a thousand children a day. From many points of view he was doing an extremely good job in an area so remote that there was little chance of the people obtaining food from any other source. At that time Achill was still cut off from the mainland; the nearest Government relief centre was at Westport, over thirty miles away, and that was already greatly over-stretched.

The trouble was that Nangle had made a great many enemies. He was a combative man, notorious for his rudeness, and rejoiced in taking the battle to the enemy. His missionaries on Clare Island are said to have stalked into a Catholic chapel, holding up a communion wafer and demanding, 'Is this your God?' Not surprisingly, they were dragged outside and severely beaten. Nangle himself did not shrink from the same kind of direct insult. He had a trenchant prose style, which he exercised to great effect in his newspaper. The front cover of the paper set the tone, with a picture of a mouse, nibbling away at the Host. For the *Achill Missionary Herald* the famine afforded a splendid opportunity for an evangelical sermon. Nangle told his readers that 'Famine is sent as a special judgement for sin' and went on to enumerate the various sins which had caused the Good Lord to inflict this calamity upon the wicked Irish Catholics, finding plenty of Biblical references to back up his words.

In 2 Sam. XXI.l., for instance, he asserted that the three-year famine had been visited upon the Israelites because Saul had slain the Gibeonites and had failed to atone for his sin. Nangle found the Irish nation guilty of the same sin, because so many murders went unpunished and so few Irishmen could be found to bear righteous witness against their fellow countrymen. In his 24 February 1847 edition, he pounced upon his readers:

Fellow countrymen – Surely God is angry with this land. The potatoes would not have rotted unless He sent the rot into them … God is good, and because He is, He never sends a scourge upon His creatures unless they deserve it – but he is so good that He often punishes people in mercy; when he sees them going in a bad way He chastises them…

And much, much more of the same kind of spiritual blackmail, but according to Nangle, the Lord's wrath was most provoked by what he saw to be the cardinal sin of the Catholics, the sin of idolatry. In another edition the evangelical mouse took a hefty bite of the consecrated Host:

> What is the object of worship in the Mass but a morsel of flour blended with water, and moulded into a wafer by the hands of man? It is just as true of the millions of Ireland as it was of the millions of Judah; 'They worship the work of their own hands, that which their fingers have made.'

This naturally infuriated the Roman Catholic clergy. While some of them might have agreed, on slightly different theological grounds, that the famine was a visitation upon the people for their sins, they would not have included idolatry among them. John McHale, the redoubtable Archbishop of Tuam, was particularly outraged by the Protestant colony's schools, which he saw as unadulterated souperism. In one of his sermons, delivered at the nearby town of Newport, he made it clear what he thought of Nangle. 'There is no place out of Hell,' he stormed, 'which more enrages the Almighty than the Protestant colony.' One of McHale's acolytes, Monsignor Hughes, went even further:

> I give you my advice, that when you meet the Jumpers or Preachers you put the sign of the Cross between yourselves and them: and as for the children you send to their school, it would be better for you if you cut their throats with a knife, for when they are in Hell, they will call upon God to put seven times more punishment upon you, their fathers and mothers, for letting them go to such schools.

Following such counter-blasts from the Church, Nangle's converts were abused by Catholic neighbours and some of them were even attacked, but Nangle himself delighted in attacks from the Roman Catholic clergy. It was all ammunition for his newspaper, but his methods and his manner were so objectionable that he made Protestant enemies as well. Mr and Mrs Hall, who were well

known for their writings about rural Ireland, criticized his harsh treatment of a pupil at one of his schools who was rash enough to fall out with his master. The boy was stripped of the clothing he had been given and turned out in rags on the road, with only three shillings in his pocket, to make the long journey home to Sligo, nearly eighty miles away. The American traveller, Asenath Nicholson, was disgusted by the stinginess with which Nangle and other evangelical missionaries treated their converts:

A 'soup' school on the west coast of Ireland in 1850. Protestant evangelists set up missions in remote areas to try to convert the Roman Catholic population. They gave the children a free meal every day and this led to charges of 'souperism' from outraged Roman Catholic clergy.

I had looked into the cabins of many of the converts in Dingle and Achill, and though their feet were washed cleaner, their stools scoured whiter, and their hearths swept better than many in the mountain cabins, yet their eightpence a day will never put shoes upon their feet, convert their stools into chairs, or give them any better broom than the mountain heath to sweep their cabins. It will never give them the palatable, well-spread board around which their masters sit and which they have earned for them by their scantily paid toil.

The great majority of Church of Ireland clergy shared this distaste for the methods of the evangelicals. Over the years, most parsons, especially those in country areas, had sought to disassociate themselves from the old evils of tithes and penal laws. They played down the doctrinal differences between Church of Ireland teachings and those of the Roman Catholics. They were latitudinarians, happy to put what they shared in common with other Christians above disputes on points of dogma. In remote areas, the priest and the parson were often the only educated men in the district and sought each other's company. There is even a well-attested story of a priest supplying his friend with a much larger congregation of quiet spectators when the Church of Ireland bishop came visiting. To such broad churchmen, violent attacks on Roman Catholic doctrine were anathema. They knew that wherever the Church was attacked, social disorder would follow, and such influence as they themselves could exert in the community would be severely compromised.

During the famine, priest and parson often worked closely together, but the spiritual duties of the priest with his huge and far-scattered flock, were often far too demanding for him to get involved with the mechanics of famine relief. Apart from anything else, there was the enormous burden of administering the last rites to far too many of his people. The Church of Ireland rector was frequently the agent who organized the distribution of food. Charities such as the British Association and the Society of Friends worked through the Church of Ireland clergy throughout the stricken areas. The great majority of the parsons who had this duty thrust upon them accepted it gladly and gave out food without distinction between Protestant and Catholic. In fact, many of them gave their lives in the process.

The harm done by the evangelicals now became apparent. On the Belmullet peninsula in Mayo and the Dingle peninsula in Kerry, around Toomore and Goleen in Cork, and in many other places where soupers had been active, people had been warned by the Roman Catholic clergy to avoid them. It was not always possible for unsophisticated people to distinguish between those who gave food with spiritual conditions attached, and those who gave it freely. Their own clergy, resentful of the attacks which had been made on them by the evangelicals, did not always help the people to make the distinction as clearly as they might have done. In many places there was bitterness and acrimony between the two faiths and it was the poor, as always, who suffered and died, rather than turn 'jumper' or 'take the soup'.

Fortunately, this was not everywhere the case. Many people kept their spiritual fingers crossed and took the soup anyway. Some made a little private pact with God, promising to return to the True Faith once the present emergency was over. And in the great majority of places the issue did not exist, even when the evangelicals were only just down the road.

In the little town with the unhappy name of Schull, usually rendered as 'Skull' in English at the time, there was a Church of Ireland vicar named Robert Traill. Toomore, where the evangelical rector, William Fisher, guarded his converts and railed against the evils of Popery, was only a few miles away. Traill also had a small congregation of Protestants, many of them just as poor as the Roman Catholics in his parish, but, unlike his neighbour, he ministered even-handedly to both. 'Frightful and fearful is the havoc around me,' Traill wrote, at the end of January 1847. 'The children in particular are disappearing with awful rapidity, and to this I add the aged who … are almost without exception swollen and ripening for the grave.'

James Mahoney, reporting for the *Illustrated London News,* drew a picture of Traill visiting the house of a man dying of fever. The man's wife was already dead and his three children were in a desperate state. In the picture the vicar cut a rather formal and detached figure, but his writings suggest that he was more compassionate than he looked. In February, Traill received a visit from a Captain Caffin, who had delivered a shipload of meal, the gift of the British Association. Caffin was shocked by what he saw in Schull and wrote a letter which was later published in *The Times.* 'Famine exists to a frightful degree with all its horrors! Fever has sprung up in consequence upon the wretchedness; the swellings of limbs and the body, and diarrhoea, from the want of nourishment, is every-where.' Traill himself was to die of fever just two months later.

Caffin's letter was received with horror in London. Even Trevelyan said he was shocked. The sad truth is that government officials often ignored the desperate appeals of their own counterparts in Ireland, because they believed that the Irish always exaggerated everything. A sober English naval officer was more difficult to ignore. However, the Government eventually succeeded in doing so. When help came, it was again from a member of the Church of

The Reverend Robert Traill, his wife Anne and the small town of Schull (at the time rendered Skull in English) where he was vicar. The town suffered exceptionally high casualties from hunger and disease. Like many Church of Ireland vicars, Traill gave his life helping the poor.

Ireland clergy, the Reverend F. Trench, a curate from County Tipperary. Trench consulted with Dr Traill and the local doctor and proposed the establishment of 'eating houses' – perhaps a way of getting round the dreaded word 'soup' – to serve the poor with stirabout. Within a month, he had recruited his cousin, Richard Chenevix Trench, Professor of Divinity at King's College, London, and the two men were running nine eating houses around Ballydehob and Schull. With the help of local volunteers each house was able to feed about 500 people a day, but Trench himself admitted that even in their own district there were 'vast regions, yet untouched'.

The success of charitable efforts such as these eventually registered with the British Government, but not until uncounted thousands of people had died and the Public Works had reached almost absurd dimensions. Because there was no other Government relief available, local committees ended up taking on anyone who could hold a shovel, men, women, the elderly, even children.

In October 1846 only 114 000 were employed, all of them men. By January 1847 the numbers had swollen to 570 000 and by March they had reached the extraordinary total of 750 000, which meant that up to three million people were dependent on this one form of relief, however inadequate and inefficient it might be. It was also extremely expensive. By the time the Works were wound up in April, Trevelyan reckoned that famine relief had cost the British tax-payer more than seven million pounds. Soup kitchens offered a cheaper and a far more effective alternative. The Soup Kitchen Act became law in January 1847, but nearly four months were to elapse before it came into full effect and in the meantime the poor continued to die.

In the end, it was not hunger alone which killed most of the people, but fever. Doctors at the time often found it difficult to determine the precise cause of death, and most patients would have suffered from a combination of several different diseases. The biggest killer, however, was almost certainly typhus. Typhus is spread by lice. It was endemic in Ireland and there were always a few sufferers among the poor, but in famine conditions the people gathered together from far and wide to seek relief. Many of them had pawned their clothes to buy food and had nothing but the rags they stood up in. They picked up lice from their neighbours in the soup kitchens or on the Public Works and had no chance of washing or changing their clothes to rid themselves of the infestation. Lice, in any case, resist a simple washing and the rags would need to be boiled to destroy them. Of course no one at the time realized the connection between lice and disease, so the infection spread, unhindered. Typhus induces a violent headache, a very high fever, grossly swollen glands and, sometimes, a blackening of the face and body which filled people with special dread. It killed two in three of those it infected.

There was another closely related disease, also louse-borne and now known as relapsing fever. The patient appears to recover, then runs a second, a third, even a fourth bout of very high fever which frequently ends in death. Doctors at the time had no way of distinguishing between the two diseases and referred to both as fever. Ironically, because both diseases flourished wherever people congregated in large numbers, workhouse infirmaries and fever hospitals intended for the treatment of disease only increased the dangers of cross-infection. In the case of typhus, the dried excreta of an infected louse turn to dust, easily become airborne and can be inhaled by anyone who happens to be nearby. Doctors visiting the sick, Church of Ireland clergymen doling out soup and Roman Catholic priests administering the last rites were often infected and many of them died. In fact middle-aged, middle-class people were more likely to die than the starving people they cared for, because the poor had often acquired some resistance by contracting mild forms of the disease in childhood.

Children did not so easily die from typhus. In their case, the biggest killer was dysentery. Again, doctors had no way of distinguishing between different forms of this disease and the cause of death was often given as 'diarrhoea'. Polluted water was of course the commonest means of transmission, so dysentery also flourished wherever too many people were using the same water supply. At the time many believed it was caused by eating Indian corn, but this was most likely either because the person handling the food was infected, or because the meal had not been properly cooked, merely steeped in cold polluted water. As people grew weaker they no longer had the strength to cut and carry turf for their fires; uncooked food and cold cabins added to their misery and hastened their deaths. Because starvation weakens resistance to infection, it is rarely possible to distinguish between one cause of death and another, but disease is usually reckoned to have killed ten times as many people as hunger alone.

Although even the most learned doctors knew little about the causes of disease, everyone knew, or thought they knew, that fever and illness generally was infectious and could be transmitted from the sick to the healthy. The sad effect of this was that people who fell ill in their cabins were often left to die unattended. A nation famous for its traditions of hospitality now closed its doors against the poor and few people could be induced to touch those who had died. Cabins where the occupants had perished were often tumbled over their heads. Corpses lay unburied.

On a visit to the Isle of Arran More off the coast of Donegal, Asenath Nicholson made another chilling entry in her journal:

> Six men, beside Mr Griffith, crossed with me in an open boat, and we landed, not buoyantly, upon the once pretty island. The first that called my attention was the death-like stillness – nothing of life was seen or heard, excepting occasionally a dog. These looked so unlike all others I had seen among the poor – I unwittingly said – 'How can the dogs look so fat and shining here, where there is no food for the people?' 'Shall I tell her?' said the pilot to Mr Griffith, not supposing that I heard him. That was enough.

Asenath Nicholson had both heard and understood. The living did not even have the strength to bury the dead where the dogs could not reach them.

During the early spring of 1847 the price of grain fell dramatically, as Trevelyan's long-awaited market forces began to have an effect. The meal which had cost three shillings a stone in February was soon on sale at half the price. Now, at last, those who were lucky enough to be both alive and in work could buy just enough to feed their families. The Government now chose to close down the Public Works, not all at once, but gradually, all over the country. Trevelyan expected farmers to hire labourers for the spring sowing, but most farmers in the worst-hit areas were watching every penny themselves. They preferred to put their fields down to grass and their money in the bank. They would not grow grain, because grain prices were falling, thanks to the abolition of the Corn Laws and cheap imports from the United States. They would not let land for conacre because they feared the return of blight, which would mean the poor cottiers would have nothing with which to pay them. Poor people had nowhere to turn but the workhouse. These had never been intended to cater for the multitudes who now begged and prayed for admission.

Government regulations forbade the distribution of food outside the workhouse gates – or outdoor relief, as it was called – so the buildings were filled to overflowing. Fever had broken out, the infirmaries and fever hospitals were full, sometimes with two and even three people to a bed, and the administration of many workhouses had collapsed under the strain. Government inspectors found conditions in some of them so bad that the Poor Law Commissioners recommended the dismissal of the masters and matrons concerned. The main problem, apart from sheer overcrowding, was that most of the workhouses could not pay their bills.

The workhouses were funded by their Poor Law unions out of the rates levied on the local residents. It was up to the Board of Guardians in each union to decide how much each householder should pay by setting a rate and collecting it from the individuals concerned. Rates were levied as a proportion of the annual income from a given piece of property and the rate was set, or 'struck' by the Guardians, according to the annual budget which they worked out for themselves. One year it might be a few pence in the pound, another year several shillings. In these desperate times, rates were obviously higher than ever before, but the main difficulty was in collecting the money. In theory, half the rate was paid by the occupier of the property, half by the landlord, but many of the smaller tenants were close to starvation themselves, many more were penniless and there were countless defaulters. A high proportion of the landlords also avoided paying rates, especially if they were absentees and could not be traced by the local Guardians, and this placed an added burden on those who paid up.

The Guardians sent out rate collectors, who were empowered to seize livestock, furniture, anything of value to pay the debt. Even so, they had an almost impossible job. To take one instance, in Lowtherstown, County Fermanagh, a collector named Thomas Robinson lodged a total of eighty-seven pounds in May 1847, a fraction of the eight-hundred pounds he was empowered to collect. In June he seized some cows from one defaulter, but the farmer's men beat him up and forcibly repossessed the cattle. He then had to put up with verbal abuse from a priest who told him that he should not be collecting at all at such a time. In October he was attacked again and was lucky to escape with his life. Some other collectors were not so fortunate. Many unions complained that the rates could not be collected, whatever methods were used. The Poor Law Commission's response was to dissolve the Board of Guardians, as it did at Lowtherstown, replace them with paid officials called vice-guardians, and send in soldiers to help collect the rates.

At this stage the Government was investing directly in only one form of relief and that was the soup kitchens. At last, in the late spring of 1847, these started to operate on a massive scale, serving stirabout or bread, or a combination of the two, to everyone who applied. On the whole, these were a great success, far cheaper to operate than the Public Works. They were humiliating, because they removed all dignity from the recipients, but they prevented the poor from dying of hunger. By midsummer, three million people were being fed by the Government in the greatest national programme of famine relief which had ever been seen. During the summer of 1847, mortality declined all over the country. If the Government had started the kitchens six months earlier, hundreds of thousands of lives might have been saved. No one can be sure of this, because fever was the biggest killer and the fever epidemic might have been even more ferocious in crowded soup kitchens than it was on the Public Works, but at least the Government would have been seen to be trying to prevent the people from starving.

Now it was to be seen doing precisely the opposite. By that remorseless irony which always seems to make bad situations worse, the whole of Britain was seized by a financial crisis in the summer of 1847. British capitalists had withdrawn vast amounts of money in gold for investment overseas. In those days, monetary theory still insisted on the gold standard and the Bank of England was not allowed to issue new notes without the gold to back them up. At the same time, many firms were urgently in need of loans to tide them over a difficult year. Unable to borrow the money to pay their debts, many firms collapsed and there was widespread recession, with workers laid off all over the country. The Government itself had difficulty meeting its commitments. There were heated debates about the state of the economy and the Chancellor of the Exchequer cast around for ways of reducing public spending.

At the same time, there was increasing indignation that so many Irish landlords seemed to be avoiding the payment of rates and neglecting to look after the
poor on their estates. The case of Lord Lucan had already been given wide publicity. The Earl of Lucan had large estates around Castlebar in County Mayo.
He had been co-operative about allowing the Poor Law Commissioners to build
a workhouse on his land, largely, it was alleged, because he believed that the
union would become bankrupt and he would gain a fine set of buildings by
default. His subsequent actions seem to have justified this slander. Lucan
himself was elected Chairman of the Board of Guardians and it can be safely
assumed that the other members of the board were more or less in his pocket.
The workhouse was three-quarters empty before the famine began, but when
crowds of frantic people tried to gain admission in October 1846, Lucan
announced that the union was bankrupt and closed the doors.

In spite of protests from the Poor Law Commissioners he refused to strike
a new rate and reopen the premises or to provide any other form of relief. The
Commissioners eventually responded by dismissing the board and installing
vice-guardians, but in the meantime, the wretched inmates of the workhouse
were allowed to starve to death. The hordes of famished people who gathered in
Castlebar were relieved only by the generosity of the townspeople. His Lordship
would have nothing to do with them. When he was called upon to explain his
conduct in the House of Lords it emerged that, although the union was owed
over a thousand pounds in rates, the chief debtor was Lucan himself. He had
refused to pay the rates on the grounds that he spent far more on his estate than
the rents brought in. The whole system, he asserted, had broken down and
needed radical reform.

This the Government now proposed to do, though the solution it had in
mind was not at all to his Lordship's taste. It was to make Irish property pay for
Irish poverty. Under the terms of the Act of Union there should have been no
major distinctions between one part of Great Britain and another, but from now
on the Government was determined that the problem of relieving the sufferings
of the Irish people was a problem for Ireland alone. In June, a new measure, the
Irish Poor Law Extension Act, was passed by the Commons. It was a piece of
legislation which was to have hideous consequences for Ireland over the next
few years.

There was little sign of disease in the potato crop in late summer and Trevelyan was convinced that the famine was over. He took his family off for a holiday in Italy, even though he had always refused to allow the same indulgence to his overworked assistants. Later in the year, he submitted, anonymously, his own account of 'The Irish Crisis' to the *Edinburgh Review* and it was published the following January. In it, Trevelyan revealed his own prejudices about the alleged idleness of the Irish peasantry, but he also made many astute observations about the shortcomings of the Irish land tenure system and its evil consequences. The most alarming aspect of the work, though, was that he seemed to see the famine itself as a Divine blessing in disguise: 'The deep and inveterate root of social evil,' he wrote, 'has been laid bare by a direct stroke of an all-wise and all-merciful Providence.' He then went on to hint at a 'sharp, but effectual remedy' which was to be all too apparent in Government policy as the Poor Law Extension Act was put into effect.

Some officials in Ireland shared Trevelyan's view that the famine was over and began to count the cost, prematurely as it turned out. The most accurate figures for mortality were compiled by a relieving officer named Marshall on the Schull peninsula in West Cork. This area was not especially remote. It was within a long day's ride from the bustling city of Cork, but it had a very high proportion of landless labourers, who had nothing to fall back on once the potatoes were gone, and the district had suffered terribly from fever. Marshall's death register recorded the name and sex of everyone who died of starvation or of famine-related diseases in six neighbouring parishes between September 1846 and September 1847. According to the 1841 census there were 43 266 people living in the district. Of these, 7332 died during the stated period. Allowing that numbers would certainly have increased by 1846 this is still a sixth of the local population who had died in just twelve months.

If those figures had been true for the whole of Ireland this would have meant the deaths of about 1 300 000 people during the same period. Fortunately, there were very many areas, especially in the north and east, where famine mortality never reached anything approaching that level, but it is quite possible that in some remote districts the numbers of dead were proportionately even greater. And for hundreds of thousands of poor Irish people the worst was yet to come.

CHAPTER FIVE

EVICTION

*I*n June 1847, with the famine still at its height and the soup kitchens feeding nearly three million people a day, Lord John Russell's government passed the Poor Law Extension Act. The Whigs were determined to put a stop to government expenditure on famine relief and transfer the whole burden of supporting Ireland's hungry millions on to the Poor Law system, even though this had never been designed to cope with famine conditions. To some extent the failure to realize that the famine was far from over is understandable. No previous subsistence crisis had lasted more than two years. Less creditably, Russell and his colleagues may also have assumed that many of those at risk had already died, or had emigrated abroad, and that the remaining poor could be catered for by reforming the existing system. Above all, they wanted to stop wasting English money on saving Irish lives.

But the Poor Law Extension Act also contained elements of deliberate social engineering. The Whig ministers in power were resolved to shape Ireland according to their own social and political preferences, and they saw the changes wrought by the famine as a splendid opportunity for doing so. The main thrust of the new legislation was aimed at ridding the country of inefficient and insolvent landlords so that agriculture could be modernized. Linked to this was the determination to transform the huge mass of poor peasantry into wage

The Poor Law Extension Act of 1847 put the whole burden of paying for relief on to the Irish landlords. Many of them turned to eviction when they were faced with ruin.

labourers, working for cash on large well-ordered farms. Trevelyan spelt out his own views in *The Irish Crisis:*

> A large population subsisting on potatoes which they raised for themselves has been deprived of that resource, and how are they now to be supported? The obvious answer is by growing something else. But that cannot be, because the small patches of land which supported a family when laid down to potatoes, are insufficient for the purpose when laid down to corn or any other kind of produce; and corn cultivation requires capital and skill which the cottier and conacre tenants do not possess. The position occupied by these classes is no longer tenable, and it is necessary for them either to become substantial farmers or to live by the wages of their labour.

The Government proposed to achieve this by making several new provisions. The most important, from the poor people's point of view, was that workhouses were now empowered to give outdoor relief to those in need, but only to those so enfeebled by age or disease that they could not possibly support themselves. The able-bodied could obtain food only by entering the workhouse itself. Moreover, relief would only be given to those who had surrendered all other means of support. Under the notorious Gregory clause, an amendment which had been introduced earlier in the year, anyone holding more than a quarter of an acre must give up his land before seeking relief. The effect of this, from the Government's point of view, would be to ensure that everyone seeking relief would be genuinely destitute, while at the same time ridding the land of 'uneconomic' smallholdings. So poor people with an acre or two of land were faced with a terrible choice between surrendering the land and heading for the workhouse, which meant giving up homes, pride, and their only hope of ever being self-sufficient, or holding on to the land and facing starvation for themselves and their children.

The Gregory clause led to fearful injustice and abuse. Many people preferred to starve to death rather than give up their land. Some of the cleverer wives took their children to the workhouse and claimed that their husbands had abandoned them, when in fact the men were hiding out in their own cabins.

*Above: 'The Discovery of the Potato Blight' by Daniel
McDonald c.1852. Potatoes often appeared to be sound when
lifted but were later found to have rotted in store, with
disastrous consequences for the poor people who depended
on them.
Overleaf: 'Evicted' by Lady Butler, 1890 – a highly
sentimentalized painting of the aftermath of eviction.
Public revulsion at scenes like this helped to bring about land
reform in Ireland.*

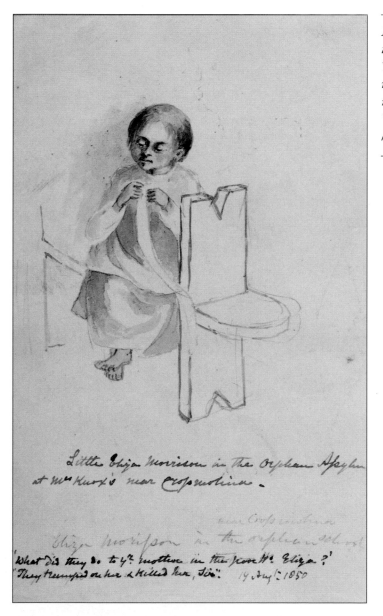

Eliza Morrison, an orphan child taken to a Protestant mission. The lower part of the inscription reads: 'What did they do to your mother in the poorhouse, Eliza?' 'They trampled on her and killed her, Sir.'

Left: 'An Irish emigrant landing at Liverpool', by Erskine Nicol, 1871. Although painted later in the century, this picture gives a Victorian perception of the way that city dwellers took advantage of immigrants. Young ruffians jeer at the man, while a nervous young woman is seeking directions behind him.

Previous pages: 'Emigrants at Cork' in 1840. Before the famine, and to some extent even during its height, many emigrants were from relatively prosperous families.
Above: Ships in quarantine at Grosse Ile, near Quebec; watercolour by H.H. Manvers Percy (1817–77). The gun battery was to persuade vessels carrying the sick to drop anchor.

Incidents like this, of course, only confirmed the authorities in the belief that the poor were incorrigible liars and made them stick more firmly to the rules. In one case, in Parsonstown, now Birr, in County Offaly, the local doctor found a woman in her cabin boiling up a hedgerow weed, charlock, to feed her hungry children. The woman's husband was in prison for debt and she had no other food to give them. Parsonstown was not in an area which had been very badly hit and such a degree of deprivation was unusual. Appalled, the doctor took the children to the workhouse and insisted on their being admitted. The matter was brought up at the next meeting of the Board of Guardians and the Chairman castigated the doctor for acting improperly. The children's father was tenant of nearly two acres, not less than a quarter. The fact that he was in prison for debt and the children were starving was immaterial. They should not have been admitted. Fortunately, the matter was not brought up again and it appears that the case was quietly forgotten, but in the poorer unions of the west it would have gone hard with those children.

The Gregory clause was not the worst aspect of the new legislation. Under the new act, in addition to liability for his own rates, the landlord also became responsible for the rates of all tenants with a holding worth less than four pounds a year. This gave the landlord an immediate interest in getting rid of his smaller tenants and consolidating his land. 'Efficient' landlords would do so by evicting as many of their tenants as they could, or by arranging for them to emigrate, and paying their fares if necessary. Those who did this would keep their estates intact and might even make them profitable. Those who did not might have to pay the rates for hundreds of impoverished tenants and might well end up by losing everything they possessed. Again, the Government's intention was plain enough. It wanted to get shot of sub-divided estates and insolvent landlords, who were regarded as negligent and inefficient.

In fact, although there were other arrogant bullies like Lord Lucan, and many more who evaded their responsibilities by skulking abroad, Irish landlords were often in genuine difficulties. The mismanagement of previous owners accumulated from one generation to the next. Under the existing laws, a landlord could not sell his estate as long as parts of it were mortgaged or otherwise 'encumbered' with debt, even if the debt repayments, plus the rates due on the estate, exceeded the income from rent. There were many such loss-making estates in Ireland and this, of course, was one reason why so many landlords were negligent and failed to pay the rates or take care of their tenants.

When Major Denis Mahon inherited Strokestown Park, in County Roscommon, just as the famine began, it was not mortgaged, but it had been in the hands of the notoriously inefficient Court of Chancery for many years. During that time no rents had been collected, sub-division had been allowed to spread unchecked and thousands of impoverished people were now struggling for survival on the land. The estate was thirty thousand pounds in debt – between one and a half and three million in today's money. Mahon knew he would be liable for heavy expenditure for the ratepayers' share of the cost of the Public Works in the neighbourhood. He was also expected to subscribe to the local relief commission. Meanwhile, none of his 1600 tenants were paying any rent and most of them were many years in arrears. To make matters worse the tenants had formed a 'combination' – a secret pact – against the payment of rent, on the familiar grounds that alien landlords had no real right to the land. One man who had offered to pay had been told he would be burned to death by 'Molly Maguire' if he paid a penny of the money he owed.

At a loss to know what to do the Major approached his cousin, John Ross Mahon, a shrewd and hard-headed businessman, who agreed to act as his agent. Ross Mahon's assessment of the estate was bleak. The only way to make it pay, he said, was to reduce the number of tenants by two thirds, thereby increasing the average size of the farms from three acres to nine, and turn the land over to the cultivation of grain. Perhaps knowing that his cousin would not agree to ruthless evictions, Ross Mahon proposed that the tenants should be persuaded to emigrate to Canada, all expenses paid, at a cost of twenty-four thousand pounds, Major Mahon would have to borrow the money and he dithered for some months over the plan. When he eventually agreed, tenants who would volunteer to emigrate were not hard to find – 490 went off in May 1847 and another 416 in June. Ross Mahon accompanied the emigrants to Liverpool and gave each individual a few pounds of rice, oatmeal and salt fish in addition to the small ration legally required of the shipping company.

In the event, the emigrants suffered terribly on the voyage and many died of fever on board the ships carrying them to the New World, but details of this could not have been known when Major Mahon returned from England to

Major Denis Mahon, owner of Strokestown Park Estate in County Roscommon. He paid for large numbers of his tenants to emigrate to Canada in order to avoid paying their rates, and was assassinated in 1847.

attend a meeting of the Strokestown Relief Committee. Here, he was unwise enough to fall out with the parish priest, Father McDermott, accusing him of playing fast and loose with the accounts. The priest was outraged and abused Major Mahon in return. There was a furious row which seems to have caused the Major deep disquiet and there were rumours that, following the dispute, Father McDermott denounced the landlord from the pulpit of his church. Two months later, Mahon went to a meeting of the Board of Guardians in Roscommon. Like many other unions in the west it was deeply in debt and the workhouse was threatened with closure. The Major attended to see if some way could be found of rescuing it. As he walked home, he was ambushed and shot dead.

Bonfires were lit throughout the neighbourhood as some of Major Mahon's tenants celebrated the news of his death. The 'Molly Maguires' were quick to claim responsibility and to threaten Ross Mahon, and several neighbouring landlords with a similar fate. Five more Irish landlords were in fact shot dead within the next few months. Three men, who may or may not have been guilty, were charged with the Major's murder and two of them were subsequently hanged. Hundreds of poor people turned out to support the alleged culprits when the executions were carried out. The whole affair attracted enormous publicity and there were accusations in the British press that Father McDermott had incited the assailants to murder Major Mahon. McDermott's bishop wrote letters in his defence, but there was further embarrassment when it came out that the bishop's own brother was a big tenant on the Strokestown estate and had himself evicted many of his sub-tenants. No one came out of the affair with clean hands.

The people who gained most from the assassination of landlords, or threats against their lives, were the strong farmers, the bigger tenants who might hope to scare their landlord into abating their rents, or suspending them altogether until the famine was over. The poor gained nothing at all. In response to what it perceived as increasing rural unrest the Government brought in the Crime and Outrage Act, which enabled the Lord Lieutenant to draft in extra police to disturbed areas at the expense of the ratepayers concerned. Extra troops were also sent to Ireland (the Government always seemed to be able to find money for the army) and a troop of dragoons was stationed at Strokestown. The presence of the soldiers made it much easier for Ross Mahon, and other agents like him, to push ahead with evictions. Ross Mahon went on to evict hundreds of families and then embarked on a prosperous career as co-founder of the Guinness-Mahon bank.

In the summer of 1847 the potato blight did not return with its former virulence and some of the few farmers who had planted their land were able to dig a good harvest, but the total acreage under potatoes was only a quarter of what it had been before the famine. Farmers who had taken on conacre tenants had received no rent in 1846 and had not re-let for the new season. Others, who had once employed labourers, had long since laid them off. When the soup kitchens were closed in October 1847 the poor had less means of support than ever before. Now, landlords in those areas like Clare, Galway and Mayo, where there were a great number of very small holdings, began to search their rent rolls for defaulters so that they could evict them. With so many in desperate need, it was not hard to find tenants who had failed to pay the rent. Very soon there were hundreds of thousands of homeless people, without food, without hope, crowding at the workhouse doors and wandering the winter roads of Ireland.

Some landlords were far more heartless than the unfortunate Major Mahon. Mr Walshe, a landlord in Crossmolina, County Mayo, had a large but unproductive estate in the remote district of Erris on the Belmullet peninsula. It was one of those places, not unlike Lord George Hill's estate in Donegal, where vast numbers of people crowded along the coastline and survived with very little interference from their landlord until the famine. The estate included three large villages and few, if any, of the inhabitants had paid any rent for many years. In the circumstances it was simple for Walshe to obtain a warrant to evict them, especially since he was the magistrate who issued the warrants. As was his right, he called upon a company of the 49th Regiment to help him and the soldiers descended on the village of Mullaroghe a few days before Christmas, 1847, where 102 families – 500 people or more – were living. Mr Walshe's men, backed up by the soldiers, drove them from their homes and pulled down their cottages. 'It would have pitied the sun,' said a local woman, 'to look at them, as they had to go, head foremost under hail and storm.' The officer in command of the army detachment was so disgusted that he found urgent reasons for declining orders to return to the site and finish the job a few days later.

Incidents such as this prompted the Prime Minister, Lord Russell, to remark: 'It is quite true that landlords in England would not like to be shot like hares and partridges … but neither does any landlord in England turn out fifty persons at once and burn their houses over their heads.' Since it was Russell's own legislation which was doing so much to increase the rate of eviction, the remark only serves to emphasize the huge gap between perceptions of the famine in London and those in Ireland itself. Russell, like Trevelyan, imagined that surplus tenants could be taken on as resident labourers, ignoring the fact that there was already a huge surplus of agricultural labourers in Ireland, but Russell could afford to be self-righteous in his ignorance. It was the officials charged with executing the Government's policy on the spot who so often found their task both distasteful and ill-conceived.

Captain Kennedy, a Poor Law Inspector from County Down, was posted to Kilrush in County Clare. In November 1847, he made his first report to the Commissioners:

The admission to the workhouse amounted to nearly 200 in the past week. Such a tangled mess of poverty, filth and disease as the applicants presented, I have never seen. Numbers in all stages of fever and small pox mingled indiscriminately with the crowd and all clamoured for admission. Their misery and utter helplessness baffles description. I was in the house from 11 am to 6.30 pm and returned to my lodgings covered with vermin. Paper could not convey the horrors and misery concentrated among two hundred persons …

Captain Kennedy was well aware of the reasons for this sudden influx of paupers. The Chairman of the Board of Guardians, and by far the biggest proprietor in the area, was Colonel Crofton Moore Vandeleur. Prior to the famine he was considered a fairly good landlord, as landlords go. His father had given the land and helped to pay for the construction of the Catholic church in Kilrush. He himself had been a conscientious chairman and had helped to defray some of the costs in the early days of the workhouse. Now he was faced with the full implications of the Poor Law Extension Act. His land was let in

Above: An evicted family in Glenbeigh, 1888. Entire communities were destroyed by eviction or 'extermination' as it was then called. Hundreds of thousands of people were forced to leave their homes and many of them died as a result.
Left: Bailiffs used battering rams to force entry. Evictions on some estates continued until the late 1890s.

hundreds of tiny parcels to poor tenants, many of whom had not paid rent, some of them for several years. With no rents coming in and huge sums in rates to pay, Vandeleur faced ruin. That November, he made up his mind to get rid of as many of his tenants as possible.

By the time Kennedy arrived, 6000 notices to quit had already been issued in the Kilrush union. To do his dirty work Vandeleur hired Marcus Keane, who was agent for a number of Clare landowners and also a landlord in his own right. Keane had a fearsome reputation. He was said by one of the local newspapers, the *Limerick Reporter*, to be 'only happy when exterminating'. He was a native Irish speaker from an ancient local family, and he had known the people of Clare from his infancy. He had the power to inspire terror in his victims in a way that few Anglo-Irish could achieve, however hard they might try.

Keane made short work of evictions. Armed with a warrant from the local magistrate and a gang of hired thugs, he would march up to the cabin door and demand that the occupants leave immediately. He gave them just enough time to collect a few possessions and then his thugs took crowbars and levers to the roof. With a few expert tugs on the bar the fragile beams collapsed. The demolition men then kicked in the walls and 'tumbled' the cottage in a matter of minutes. The tears of the children and the pleadings of the women had no effect. As soon as the wretched people were out on the road, they were forbidden to return to the ruins of their house and everyone else on the estate was forbidden to take them in, on pain of eviction themselves. If evicted families stayed on the estate, they might have remained a charge on the land-lord's rates.

Marcus Keane was only one, though perhaps the most notorious, of the many agents carrying out work of this kind in different parts of Ireland. On the Dingle peninsula in County Kerry there was a Catholic woman, named Bess Wright, who evicted hundreds of people from Lord Cork's estate. She was so hated that when she died, many years later, a group of her former victims went to dance on her grave. Marcus Keane himself was to meet with a similar posthumous act of vengeance. His body was exhumed from the grave and flung on a dung heap. For the time being, however, these were the people in effective power, with the landlords behind them, pushing them on to do their worst. The starving army of evicted people thronged the roads of Ireland, drifting from place to place, finding almost all doors locked against them, seeking refuge in ditches, under rocks, in pathetic shelters called *scalps* or *scalpeens*, which they built for themselves. Uncounted thousands of them died. Others, with less pride perhaps, or more optimism, turned first to the workhouse.

In Kilrush union, a deeply angry Captain Kennedy did what he could to clean up the workhouse and make it fit for the hundreds of applicants who now begged for admission, but he was only a paid official, not one of the elected guardians, and his powers were limited. He managed to persuade the workhouse matron to separate the fever patients from the relatively healthy inmates and enforce some kind of quarantine. By interceding with his employers, the Poor Law Commissioners, he also succeeded in getting the elderly master of the workhouse dismissed, but he was unable to prevent the Board of Guardians from appointing the old man's son in his place. Frustrated by the regulations limiting his powers, Kennedy took to sending long reports to the Commissioners, documenting everything that went on in the union, even when there was nothing he could do about it.

Between November 1847 and July of the following year he recorded the eviction of 900 families, totalling 4000 people. Their houses were levelled and they were forced to leave the estate. Everyone knew that most of those evicted faced almost certain death. Many years later, when staying as a guest of Lord Carnarvon, Kennedy remembered these events with cold rage:

> I can tell you, my Lord, that there were days in that western country when I came back from some scene of eviction so maddened by the sights of hunger and misery I had seen in the day's work, that I felt disposed to take the gun from behind my door and shoot the first landlord I met.

In December, there were so many people in need of food and shelter that large crowds had gathered at the workhouse gates. When they were denied admission, the men demanded outdoor relief. When this too was refused they rioted and tried to break into the workhouse stores. Kennedy was attacked, but with the help of the workhouse staff he succeeded in confining his assailant in the lock-up. Eventually a troop of soldiers arrived and order was restored,

This 1850s photograph shows a group of British Army officers as they would have looked at the time of the famine. Many of them found the task of standing by at evictions distasteful.

but only by admitting an additional 300 people into the premises. Kilrush workhouse, like many others up and down the country, was not simply over-crowded. It was overflowing.

This was not due to an excess of charity. In December 1847 the Government relaxed one of the provisions of the Poor Law Extension Act, allowing outdoor relief to be given to able-bodied workers if there was no other provision available. There were thousands of starving people on the streets of the town, but as long as there were places inside the workhouse, outdoor relief could legally be refused. It was cheaper to care for the limited number of paupers who applied for admission into the workhouse than to feed the thousands who thronged the streets, so it was in the Guardians' interests to keep some spare capacity within the workhouse gates. Instead of the 800 paupers for which it had been built, Kilrush workhouse harboured as many as 5000 people several times during the famine and the Guardians rented a former hotel and several houses for extra accommodation. That December, Captain Kennedy himself took over a former pig slaughterhouse as a temporary fever hospital.

This building quickly acquired an evil reputation. In one week 99 patients out of 101 in the hospital died. In another, 75. The name 'slaughterhouse' had a new and dreadful resonance for the inhabitants of Kilrush and they avoided entering the workhouse for as long as they could. But one potent reason remained. Paupers who died within the walls were usually buried in a coffin. Those who died in the street were simply wrapped in a shroud, or an old shawl, or even in straw before being dumped in a mass grave. The people were torn between dread of the workhouse and dread of being buried without a coffin, so many entered the premises only when they had lost all hope of survival, just to be sure of getting a few flimsy boards for themselves. In widely separated unions, including Lurgan in prosperous County Armagh, this was the reason given for the hideously high mortality rate in the workhouse.

By mid-February 1848, the Kilrush union was feeding nearly 10 000 people on outdoor relief. The Guardians took over a warehouse on the quay and turned it into a vast soup kitchen with boilers constantly on the go, cooking up stirabout and dishing it out to the hungry people. Kilrush now faced another problem. The Guardians had run out of money. They had been unable, or unwilling, to collect sufficient rates to pay their bills and the tradesmen who supplied the workhouse with food and clothing refused to allow them any more credit. The Poor Law Commissioners then dissolved the Board of Guardians and appointed two vice-guardians in their place.

This was not at all unusual. The previous autumn, Lord Clarendon, Lord Lieutenant of Ireland, had warned the British Government that only eight out of the 130 unions in the country had any money in hand. He further advised that the Poor Law Extension Act would put an additional burden on their resources, which they would find impossible to support. Trevelyan thought he knew better. It was just a matter of forcing the ratepayers to stump up. The Poor Law Commissioners suspected, rightly in some cases, that locally-elected Guardians, often landlords themselves, would be unlikely to tax themselves or their neighbours more than they had to. So when a union got into debt the Commissioners invariably appointed vice-guardians, with instructions to strike a new rate, always higher than before, and to make sure that it was collected. Despite its austerity programme, the Government was always willing to send in troops to back them up. So large a number of soldiers were sent to Mayo that some observers reckoned it cost three times as much to collect the rates as they were worth.

At the beginning of 1848 the British Government was less concerned with the problems of Poor Law unions in the west of Ireland than it was with the wave of revolution which was beginning to engulf the whole of Europe. That spring, there were insurrections in Berlin, Milan, Venice, Vienna, and even in Serbia. On 22 February the rebels seized Paris and King Louis Philippe was forced to take refuge in England. French revolutionaries were advancing a radical political programme for the new Second Republic. In the words of the *Illustrated London News:*

> It insists not merely upon civil and religious liberty, and in a share of Government, through the suffrage, for the whole adult male population, but upon new social relations between wealth and labour. It is in fact Socialism, or Communism; and insists that the State can and must supply food and labour for the whole population.

Ideas like these were echoed by the Chartists, a popular protest movement which was gathering momentum in England itself. The Chartists were led by an Irish landlord, Fergus O'Connor. They demanded universal male suffrage, voting by ballot and a comprehensive programme of democratic reform. O'Connor also had a Utopian vision which was deeply attractive to many English industrial workers. He set up co-operatives to buy large farms, which were then split up into smallholdings of three or four acres which workers could rent from the National Land Company. Ironically few members of the new agricultural settlements would pay any rent and O'Connor went bankrupt. In the spring of 1848, however, the Chartists mounted a huge demonstration on Kennington Common. They planned a march on Parliament to present their mammoth charter, but the bridges across the Thames were blocked by a large force of special constables, mostly middle- and upper-class volunteers, including Charles Dickens and the refugee French Emperor in waiting, Louis Napoleon.

Like Daniel O'Connell before them, the Chartists shrank from violence and the huge demonstration came to nothing.

On the Continent, the new radicals were less inhibited about violence. Their ideas found a ready audience in Ireland and the methods of the European revolutionaries provided an example of how they might be put into practice. Up to this point, very few of the leaders who had fired nationalist sentiment in Ireland had been true revolutionaries. Daniel O'Connell, despite the huge crowds which gathered to hear him, was not a radical. The programme of his Repeal movement was really no more than its name suggested – an end to the union, limited self government, and a moderate amount of reform to allow the Irish ruling class a greater say in Ireland's affairs. In reaction against this essential conservatism a group of young men calling themselves 'Young Ireland' began agitating for much more radical measures. They included Charles Gavan Duffy, son of a Catholic grocer; Thomas Meagher, a fiery advocate of armed rebellion, and John Mitchel, son of an Ulster Presbyterian minister. There was another slightly curious figure in their midst: William Smith O'Brien, scion of an ancient Irish family. He was a Protestant and a landlord, with a large estate at Cahermoyle, in County Limerick. In his absence, he was sharply criticized by an itinerant Scots journalist, William Somerville, for paying starvation wages to his labourers, clearing his estate of superfluous tenants and turning good arable land over to grass. Nevertheless, like many members of great Irish families over the years, he considered himself an Irish patriot.

Gavan Duffy was the editor of the group's newspaper, *The Nation*, which called for complete independence from Britain. Although Duffy was himself a devout Catholic, he hired the Protestant Mitchel as his chief leader writer. Editorials in *The Nation* were charged with a spirit of Irish nationalism which transcended sectarian differences with the same idealism which had inspired the United Irishmen of the late eighteenth century. At first, much of the new move-ment's energy was taken up in divisive struggles with the Repealers, led by Daniel O'Connell's son, John, and the paper's editorials avoided anything which might smack of socialism. After all, men like Smith O'Brien, with large landed estates, were not in a hurry to give it all away. At the same time, the leaders wanted to embrace as many shades of opinion as possible, so the message was simple: Ireland for the Irish.

We who preach NATIONALITY are not factionalists or partisans, but desire and devise to lead this nation out of slavery, in its unbroken integrity, with all its legitimate orders and degrees, creeds and parties intact. Whoever is for nationality, for raising Ireland to be a nation among the nations, is our confederate, and we invite his assistance. He is an Irishman who knows his duty – that is enough. If he be Protestant, we dare not insist that he walk by Catholic rules – if he is a Conservative, we do not pledge him to Radicalism or Whiggery. The fashioning of our constitution will lie with our Parliament and there let each battle for his own opinions as stoutly as he can.

Above left: William Smith O'Brien, Protestant landlord, descendant of an ancient Irish family and Irish revolutionary. He was too much of a gentleman to make an effective guerrilla. Above right: John Mitchel, Ulster Presbyterian and anti-British propagandist. Economical with the truth, he was still effective as a myth maker. Right: This Punch *cartoon of 1846 caricatures the Young Ireland party's determination to take up arms. It also reveals English prejudice against the Irish.*

YOUNG IRELAND IN BUSINESS FOR HIMSELF.

There was no outright censorship at the time and the newspaper circulated freely. One of those who read it was a lonely, crippled man named Fintan Lalor. Despite his isolation, Lalor saw that Ireland's fundamental problem was land tenure. Until Irishmen owned the land themselves, under far more equitable arrangements than could be obtained at the time, there could be no way forward. Like Trevelyan, though with a profoundly different prescription to offer, Lalor recognized that the famine had changed everything. The old way of life was no longer tenable and agrarian revolution was the only answer. Lalor made contact with the 'Young Ireland' leaders; they immediately recognized the power of his arguments and printed his articles in their newspaper.

By 1848 other writers had taken up the same themes and began to call for a 'social revolution' – for the redistribution of land, for universal male suffrage, for a society of freehold peasants in control of their own affairs. 'My remedy for the social evils of Ireland,' stormed Thomas D'Arcy M'Gee, another apostle of revolution, 'may be found in the one word RIGHTS.' The movement generated large public meetings and the call for revolution gathered force.

So far, there had been little talk of armed rebellion. The people were worn down by famine and the British Army seemed all powerful, but as the 'Young Ireland' leaders saw the apparent ease with which old tyrannies were being overthrown in Europe, they began to hear the call to arms. Mitchel, whose hatred for Britain knew no bounds, was so incensed by his colleagues' caution that he broke away from them and launched his own paper, the *United Irishman*. In it, he published instructions for the manufacture of home-made bombs and called on his readers to attack British officials and soldiers whenever they saw the chance. He was a master of passionate invective, so passionate that he himself became carried away by the power of his own rhetoric and was soon demanding all-out war against the foreign oppressor, no matter what the cost.

Reluctantly at first, the other 'Young Ireland' leaders fell into line and the public meetings took on an increasingly martial tone. Government spies were everywhere and the authorities were alarmed. In March 1848 Smith O'Brien, Meagher and Mitchel, were arrested and charged with sedition, then released on bail, which gave the plotters a little time to advance their preparations for rebellion. All three men faced trial in May, but there was insufficient evidence to convict Meagher and O'Brien. Mitchel, whose fiery provocations almost insisted on his own conviction, was found guilty and sentenced to transportation to Tasmania, but the conditions were not too irksome. He was allowed to wear his own clothes and instructions were issued that 'as regards food and exercise he should have such indulgence as the state of his health might seem to require'. This does not seem to have struck either him or his captors as ironic at a time when thousands of his fellow countrymen were dying of starvation.

The Government brought in a new Treason Felony Act a few weeks later, which allowed the judiciary to try political agitators without having to follow through with a grisly execution in the event of the accused being found guilty. So long as there was no armed rebellion, the Government seemed nervous of coming down too hard on its critics and permitted a surprising amount of political turmoil, but armed rebellion was now on the way. Tens of thousands of troops were moved into positions around the country to forestall it. In July, the authorities warned that sellers and publishers of 'felonious and seditious papers' would be prosecuted. Duffy was arrested and Meagher was re-arrested shortly afterwards, but again released on bail. By this time, Smith O'Brien and the other leaders were on the move, trying to drum up support for their cause.

On 22 July, *The Nation* published a letter from Duffy, smuggled out of prison, proclaiming that Ireland was at war. The same edition carried a stirring call to arms:

> Ireland! Ireland! it is no petty insurrection – no local quarrel – no party triumph that summons you to the field. The destinies of the world – the advancement of the human race – depend now on your courage and success; for if you have *courage*, success must follow. Tyranny, and injustice, and bigotry are gathering together the chains which have been flung off by every other nation of Europe, and are striving to bind them upon us, – the ancient, brave, free, Irish people. It is a holy war to which we are called – against all that is opposed to justice, and happiness, and freedom. Conquer, and tyranny is subdued for ever.

Smith O'Brien was not in favour of actual rebellion. He believed that it would be enough to build up a network of armed 'clubs' all over the country and negotiate with the British Government from a position of strength, but when

Thomas Meagher brought news that there was a warrant out for O'Brien's arrest, he was at last persuaded that revolutionary war was the only answer.

Enthusiastic crowds greeted the 'Young Ireland' leaders wherever they went, but plans for the coming revolution were still unformed. The leaders had no money, no strategy, no guns, no military expertise. Although they did not venture into the areas of greatest destitution, there was no part of Ireland that had escaped completely from the ravages of famine and the people were in no condition for battle. On the rare occasions that Smith O'Brien succeeded in assembling a large body of men, it soon became apparent that most of them had only come in the hope that they would be fed; but O'Brien resolutely refused to allow them to commandeer food from tradesmen or farmers. When food was not forthcoming, the volunteers vanished as quickly as they had come. O'Brien himself was far too well-mannered to make an effective guerrilla leader. In the town of Mullinahone, County Tipperary, the crowd of men who gathered to hear him really were prepared to fight, but he declined to let them fell trees to make barricades, without first asking permission from the owners. He then went to the police station and demanded that the men surrender their arms. The sergeant pleaded that they would be too ashamed to surrender without putting on some show of a fight, so O'Brien tactfully withdrew to parade his forces. While his back was turned, the police promptly left town, taking their guns with them.

Having assembled large bodies of men several times, only to see them disappear, the leaders now grew discouraged and wanted to go to ground and wait for a more favourable opportunity. Smith O'Brien refused to give up. On 30 July 1848 he and his lieutenant, James Stephens, were left with a party of volunteers, variously estimated at between forty and five hundred men, who had gathered together near Ballingarry, County Tipperary. In the group about twenty had guns, and the remainder were armed with crudely-made pikes, cudgels, some of them only with stones. They were still sorting themselves out when a group of fifty constables, led by an inspector on a horse, arrived on the scene.

The affair which followed reads like the libretto from a Victorian comic opera. Alarmed by the angry crowd, the police retreated, pursued by stones and occasional shots from the excited rebels. After a mile or two, they stumbled

Widow McCormack's house – scene of the farcical showdown at the end of the 1848 rebellion.

across an isolated farmhouse belonging to a Mrs McCormack, who was a widow with seven children. She was out at the time, but her children took refuge in the kitchen while the police barricaded the doors and windows. The rebels took up positions around the house and both sides began firing at each other. The building still stands. It is solidly built of stone, with clear views to the front and sides, and the only cover for assailants at the time was a low wall around the garden and some farm buildings at the back. 'It is a question,' wrote the correspondent from the *Illustrated London News,* 'if 500 of the best-disciplined soldiers would have taken that house from 50 well-armed men.'

Whatever his other failings, Smith O'Brien was not lacking in courage and he resolved to try. Unaware of the children in the house, he sent a party to the back of the building to set fire to the outbuildings in the hope of smoking out the enemy. At this moment, Mrs McCormack returned home. She found Smith O'Brien and demanded that he halt the attack while her children were inside. O'Brien immediately stopped his men from firing the outbuildings and went forward, accompanied only by Mrs McCormack, to negotiate with the police.

To approach the house, full as it was with extremely jumpy armed men, was an act of considerable courage, but both sides seem to have suspended fire for a few minutes while O'Brien approached a window, bristling with police carbines, and offered his hand over the top of the barricade. He explained to the bewildered constables inside that he did not want to hurt them. He only wanted their guns. If they would leave their carbines behind and go quietly away he would let them go unharmed.

The police inspector was upstairs and knew nothing of this peace mission. While O'Brien was still attempting to negotiate on the windowsill, some of his more foolish supporters took matters into their own hands and hurled a volley of stones at the house. The police responded with a fusillade from the upstairs windows. One of the rebels was killed instantly and several were wounded, one seriously. The rest fled in confusion. Smith O'Brien was left to escape as best he could. He borrowed the inspector's horse, which was tied up outside, and rode away. The frightened police stayed in the barricaded house and did not emerge

The arrest of Smith O'Brien. He was taken while trying to catch a train home, preferring to risk imprisonment rather than cause trouble to anyone for sheltering him.

until the following day. By this time O'Brien was far away, but a few days later he gave himself up at Thurles railway station. He could have stayed in hiding, but he did not want to get the people who were sheltering him into trouble with the authorities. (O'Brien was tried for treason, but his sentence was commuted and he joined Mitchel in exile in Tasmania, before retiring peacefully to the Irish countryside.) So ended, in black farce, the great rebellion of 1848, but the spirit which it engendered and the ideas which inspired its more passionate advocates were not to die so easily.

While so many were weak and dispirited from hunger, most ordinary people may not have been able to find the will to fight, but by December 1848 it was obvious that the combined effects of Government policy and ruthless eviction were bringing about dreadful changes in the Irish countryside, which the people were powerless to resist. The *Tipperary Vindicator* published a solemn editorial:

> Whole districts are cleared. Not a roof-tree is to be seen where the happy cottage of the labourer or the snug homestead of the farmer at no distant day cheered the landscape. The ditch side, the dripping rain, and the cold sleet are the covering of the wretched outcast the moment the cabin is tumbled over him; for who dare give him covering from the pitiless storm? Who has the temerity to afford him the ordinary rites of hospitality, when the warrant has been signed for his extinction? There are vast tracts of the most fertile land now thrown out of tillage. No spade, no plough goes near them … The torpor and apathy which have seized on the masses are only surpassed by the atrocities perpetrated by those who set the dictates of humanity and the decree of the Almighty at equal defiance.

After three years of famine, many people could think only of saving themselves and some obviously lacked the strength even to do that. For the homeless and destitute there was no alternative but to tramp wearily into the nearest town and join the crowd around the workhouse, begging for relief; but for those with a little money and some energy, there was one other possibility of salvation. Emigration.

CHAPTER SIX

EMIGRATION

*I*n December 1846 the Marquess of Clanricarde, a prominent Irish landowner, wrote to the British Prime Minister, Lord John Russell: 'nothing can effectually and immediately save the country without an extensive emigration. And I have not met in Town or in Country, a reflecting man who does not entertain more or less the same opinion.' The reflecting men of Clanricarde's acquaintance were very likely landlords themselves and they would have seen the same advantages in clearing their overcrowded estates. Until that time they could have voiced the same sentiment for years, as some of them did, and few of their tenants would have listened unless forced into it. The difference now was that ordinary Irish men and women had come to the same conclusion, and were acting on it, in enormous numbers, with little prompting from the likes of Lord Clanricarde.

For every two or three families who stayed on their little patch of land, or besieged the workhouses in the hope of relief, there was another heading for the seaports, trying desperately to escape the twin horrors of starvation and disease. Tenants who could lay their hands on a few pounds hoped to cross the Atlantic to North America, and those who could scrape together just a few shillings could buy a passage on one of the steamers which plied across the Irish Sea to Glasgow and Liverpool. Short as the voyage was, it could be dangerous. A steamer bound from Sligo to Liverpool put into Derry with seventy-two dead

An emigrant ship. Not all vessels engaged in the trade were 'coffin ships', but conditions on board could still be appalling.

passengers. The captain had battened down the hatches during a storm and the people had suffocated in the overcrowded hold. Many people were fearful of the voyage, but terror drove them on board and the decks of all the steamers were clogged with passengers desperate to get away. There was also a regular trade carrying coal from the ports of South Wales to southern Ireland and these filthy vessels were also packed with fleeing people. There is one account, which confirms the cynicism of the Canadian timber merchants, of some paupers being transported on board colliers from Cork to Cardiff for nothing, 'because captains find it cheaper to ship and unship this living ballast than one of lime or shingle'.

There are no accurate records, but research suggests that up to 300 000 Irish people sought refuge in mainland Britain in 1847 alone. They came because they knew that poor people on the other side of the Irish Sea were not generally allowed to starve. Outdoor relief in England was given as a matter of course. If it was necessary to seek admission to the workhouse the diet was frugal, but to the poor Irish it must have seemed lavish. There were three meals a day instead of the two usual in Ireland and there was bread with every meal, tea to drink, and meat on the table at least once a week. In pursuit of these luxuries, Irish immigrants flooded into every port on the western seaboard. Once on the mainland, if they could find the strength to go on, they spread out across the country until there was hardly a town in the British Isles without a contingent of Irish beggars. Every major city already had an Irish quarter and it was always the most overcrowded and squalid slum in town. Once across the Irish Sea, few people died of hunger, but they carried the fever with them and there were outbreaks of typhus in Glasgow, Manchester, Birmingham, Cardiff, London, and many other cities up and down the country. This massive invasion of diseased paupers did little to increase English compassion for the Irish poor.

The city which received by far the biggest influx was Liverpool. In the last weeks of 1846 and the first weeks of 1847 thousands of immigrants flooded into the port. The workhouses were soon full, so they crowded into the cheap lodging houses, overflowed into the cellars, and when these too were full, they huddled together on the streets. By January 1847, 130 000 people a week were being fed on outdoor relief. In normal times, to be on the streets of Liverpool without means of support was a crime. On 28 January the town's magistrates held an emergency meeting to consider what was to be done. 'The gaols,' one said, 'might have been filled ten times over and the paupers would only have been better fed than before.' The ratepayers grew anxious about the burden imposed on their pockets. A local subscription of four thousand pounds was raised, not to feed the poor people, but to send them back to Ireland.

A COURT FOR KING CHOLERA.

A Punch *cartoon of 1852. English cities all had an Irish quarter, notorious hotbeds of poverty and disease. The massive influx of poor Irish people into England during the famine made them unpopular with the host country.*

Above: Prince Edwin Street, Liverpool, in the early 1900s. This street and many others in the area offered cheap lodging for poor Irish people and crowded conditions remained long after the first wave of immigration was over.
Previous pages: Dublin docks in the 1860s. Although steam vessels were in use from the 1790s onwards, their relatively short range and uncertain seaworthiness meant that sailing ships were used for long-haul voyages until late in the nineteenth century.

Eventually the Government agreed; several boatloads of poor Irish were returned to Dublin and the great tide of immigrants tailed off, but by that time it was too late to stop the fever. Liverpool's cheap lodging houses were infested with lice, the lice were infected with typhus, and anyone staying in those lodging houses was almost certain to contract the disease. The distinction of being a fever port – though few realized it at the time – was one which Liverpool shared with a number of Irish ports, notably Cork and Sligo, and this was to have fearful consequences for many of the luckless emigrants before their journey was done.

Some accounts of the famine emigration across the Atlantic have laid great stress on the appalling poverty of the Irish people who landed in Canada and the United States. There were paupers on some ships, especially in those comparatively rare cases where a landlord or even one of the Poor Law unions had paid for the passage. The arrival of these wretched people excited much comment and criticism on the other side of the Atlantic, but most of those who set out on the voyage were not utterly destitute, The utterly destitute died in Ireland, or at best made their way to England. All things are relative, but in Irish terms it was slightly more prosperous people, small tenant farmers, small tradesmen, or those whose relatives had sent them the money for the fare, who made up the bulk of the Atlantic emigrants. By the standards of most European countries they would certainly have been poor and many were indeed penniless by the time they had paid their fares, but in Ireland many of them were regarded as well off. In fact landlords began to lament the departure, not of the destitute whom they were hoping to be rid of, but of those whom they regarded as able-bodied and useful tenants.

The bailiffs may also have been disappointed, because many tenants sold what remained of their possessions and bolted with the money without paying rent or rates. More than one aggrieved landlord noted sourly that the corn for the rent had been standing one day, and by the next morning both corn and tenants were gone. A Quaker observer, watching emigrants go on board a ship bound for the United States, described their joy at getting away 'as though they were flying from a doomed land'. In fact the British Government had considered the possibility of paying for Irish emigration and then rejected it. In the cynical words of the Colonial Secretary, Lord Grey:

The Government cannot undertake to convey emigrants to Canada because, if it were to do so, if we were even to undertake part of the cost, an enormous expense would be thrown upon the treasury, and after all, more harm than good would be done ... some £150,000 would have to be spent in doing that which if we do not interfere, will be done for nothing.

The great majority of Irish emigrants yearned to go to the United States, land of promise and opportunity, but passage to British North America was cheaper. In 1847 fares peaked during the first wave of panic early in the year and then settled down to about four pounds for a passage to Boston or New York and three pounds for Quebec, with small children travelling at half price. There were also some emigrants able to find the fourteen pounds or so to go to Australia, sometimes to join relatives who had been sentenced to transportation and had now served their sentences and made a new life there. Some, hitherto law-abiding, citizens deliberately committed crimes in 1847 and gave themselves up in the hope that they too would be transported.

The owners of ships bound for these destinations placed advertisements in the newspapers and stuck up posters which described the vessels in reassuring terms and announced the estimated dates of departure. In the spring of 1847, the prospect of vastly increased demand brought all kinds of unscrupulous operators into the field. Colliers and other coasters, quite unfit for the Atlantic passage, and all manner of rotten hulks, including the notorious 'coffin ships', were drafted into service. There was also a great demand for officers and seamen to man these vessels and standards of recruitment fell as the demand increased.

All the ports in the British Isles, including places like Aberystwyth and Maryport, which rarely engaged in this kind of traffic, were thronged with Irish emigrants desperate for a passage. Agents and shipping companies employed 'runners', often Irish themselves, who descended on new arrivals in the ports and cajoled or bullied them into their own companies' offices. Some of the 'runners' were outright thieves, who robbed and cheated the emigrants out of their savings before they had even embarked. Inevitably, many emigrants also had to sleep for several nights in the cheap, infected, lodging houses, where a few pence bought a space on the lousy floor.

The law required that emigrants attend a medical inspection before going on board. According to eyewitnesses at the time, this was cursory to say the least. Some doctors sat in a wooden cubicle while people simply filed past them. The point was that the shipping companies had no interest in the fate of their passengers, once they had bought a ticket. It was a one-way voyage. There was no expectation that any of these people were going to return. So the most profitable course for an unscrupulous operator was to pack as many of them as possible on to a ship, with as little outlay on their comfort as the law required. The Passenger Acts stated that each emigrant should have ten cubic feet of space for himself and his baggage, a berth, sufficient drinking water for the voyage, and a daily allowance of food, usually a pound of meal or the same amount of bread or biscuit a day. Unfortunately, many owners and their captains ignored the rules, or paid them no more than lip service. The food was often mouldy and the water foul before the vessel even left port.

Passengers going on board were relieved of their heavier baggage, which was stowed elsewhere, and then shown down a dark companionway to the long gloomy space beneath the main deck, where they would be allotted their berths. These were simply spaces on wooden bunks. The bunks were usually six foot square and built into the ship's timbers on either side of the hold, with a gang-way down the middle. On larger vessels there might be room for trestle tables, or a few upturned tubs in the gangway. In the smaller ships there was not. If the hold was deep there might be two tiers of bunks, one on top of the other, which only added to the hazards. Either way, double or single, the allotted space for each adult was a quarter of one bunk, or eighteen inches of bed space. Children had to be fitted into nine inches, perhaps by turning them end to end.

There was no bedding of any kind. Passengers were usually advised to purchase a mattress before going on board, but many made do with straw and such clothing as they possessed. Before the Passenger Acts were tightened up, later in the century, men and women were herded together in the hold, and a single girl might easily find herself sharing a bunk with totally strange men. Alcohol was often freely available for those who could afford it. In some ships the captain made the sale of liquor his own private perk. Small wonder that one observer noted how passengers on the Atlantic voyage often became 'totally depraved and corrupted'.

Shortage of food affected almost everyone. The emigrants were usually advised to take their own sea store of food, as the rations specified under the Passenger Acts would not keep anyone in moderate health for more than a few weeks. Of course, very few of the famine emigrants could afford to take their own food. If they had any spare money at all they wanted to keep it to help them on their way when they landed.

Once the voyage started, the captain or the mate would usually distribute meal and water on a daily basis. Captains were sometimes dishonest and served short measures of both food and water, to say nothing of the quality of either. Passengers had to do their own cooking in a brick-lined fire box on the deck. There was rarely enough space for more than a few people at a time to cook their meals, so many passengers ended up with food that was half-cooked, or not cooked at all. Since the water was often contaminated, this meant that there were many outbreaks of dysentery on board ship. Even in the best of circumstances dysentery is an unpleasant and dangerous disease, especially for children, but conditions on the emigrant ships made it disastrous.

Seamen had always used the 'heads', a hazardous perch right up in the ship's bows, to relieve themselves. Passengers, male or female, were expected to do the same. While it is one thing for an experienced sailor to cling by his fingers to a narrow rail while lowering his trousers over a heaving sea, it is quite another for a frail landsman. Apart from any embarrassment which men and women may have felt about exposing themselves in this way, the operation was also very dangerous. For quite understandable reasons, many passengers preferred to use a bucket, or they went down into the cable tiers beneath the lower deck and immediately beneath their own accommodation. When the hatches were closed, which they often were in heavy weather, the stench in the hold must have been appalling, even without sickness on board. When dysentery broke out and people were unable to contain themselves, the conditions do not bear thinking about.

Comparisons were often made, both at the time and later, with the slave ships which had so recently made the Atlantic run, but such comparisons do not really hold true. African slaves were chained naked to the decks, unable to move more than a few inches in any direction, in far crueller conditions than those on the worst of the emigrant ships. But slaves were valuable property. When the weather allowed they were brought up on deck and forced 'to dance and sky-lark' in the open air. Frequently, they and the decks on which they lay, were hosed down with strong jets of sea water. The death rate was sometimes appalling, especially if the ship was becalmed and ran out of supplies, but slaves died most frequently from dysentery, or 'bloody flux', probably contracted from infected water or from the filth on the decks when heavy weather made hosing down impossible. Typhus was not usually a problem. The slaves were not allowed to wear clothes and rarely harboured lice.

Dysentery was also a killer on the emigrant ships, for the same reasons, but it was difficult to hose down a deck piled with luggage and clothing. The most murderous disease, in any case, was typhus. The voyage across the Atlantic took anything up to three months. The cramped living quarters in the hold, and

The crowded holds of emigrant ships made them an ideal breeding ground for lice and the typhus they carried.

the fact that people had no means of changing their clothes or their bedding, provided ideal conditions for the spread of body lice and the typhus fever they carried. If one passenger had contracted the disease before he came on board, others soon caught it. In those days typhus was often called 'ship fever' or 'gaol fever' precisely because it was so common in these overcrowded and dirty conditions. On some ships the first deaths occurred within a few days at sea and then continued to multiply as the voyage continued. On board the *Virginius*, from Liverpool, which was one of the ships carrying Major Mahon's luckless emigrants, 158 people died. The extra food they carried did them little good. The ship was infected with typhus.

In 1847, Quebec was second only to New York as the most frequent destination for the emigrant ships. Many of the passengers would have preferred

Ships in harbour at Quebec which was the main point of entry for emigrants to Canada in 1847.

to go direct to the United States, but even if they could have afforded the higher fares, New York was not then the haven for refugees which it was later to become. Most Americans were Protestant Anglo-Saxons, and while they had no love for the British, they had no intention of opening the gates to a flood of impoverished Irish Roman Catholics. All ports on the eastern seaboard of the USA demanded that the captain post a bond to ensure that his passengers did not become a charge on their rates. In 1847 these extra costs were quite enough to divert many vessels further north. Instead of sailing directly to the United States, they often deceived the emigrants into thinking that Quebec and Boston were virtually next door to one another and that it was an easy matter to slip across the border.

In their anxiety to populate the Canadian wilderness, the British authorities unintentionally provided the means for this back-door entry into the United States. They placed no restrictions on immigration and gave free passage up river to all new arrivals, but they did require all vessels with sick passengers on board to fly a yellow flag and drop anchor at a quarantine station. The master had then to land all passengers, both sick and healthy, at the station, where they would be kept in isolation until the ship had been given clearance. A gun battery on the shore made it unwise to ignore the requirement.

The quarantine station for Quebec was at Grosse Ile, one of a group of small islands in the great St Lawrence river, thirty miles downstream from the city itself. From November to April it is locked in ice, but in May the scrubby woodland which covers half the island bursts into leaf and the meadows on the northern shore are covered in wild flowers. In 1847 the men in charge of this pretty island faced the arrival of the first ships with trepidation. The previous year had brought an unusually large number of emigrants to Quebec and a larger number of people than usual had occupied the ramshackle wooden hospital sheds. Throughout the winter the local newspapers kept everyone informed about the famine in Ireland. They knew that the potato harvest had failed again that year and some of the more perceptive officials realized that thousands of people would be trying to flee the country.

Anticipating disaster, Mr Buchanan, the Chief Emigration Officer, obtained a supply of army tents. Dr Douglas, the medical officer in charge of quarantine, sought permission from the provincial government to build a new hospital on Grosse Ile. After some official quibbling permission was given, but instead of the three thousand pounds he had asked for, Dr Douglas received less than three hundred. It was nothing like enough.

The first vessel to arrive when the ice had cleared in the middle of May was the *Syria* out of Liverpool. Nine passengers had died during the voyage and there were 84 cases of fever still on board when the ship dropped anchor off Grosse Ile. Douglas reckoned that at least another 20 of the remaining 150 passengers were likely to sicken. His hospital had room for only 200 people and the very first ship had half filled it.

The *Syria* also brought news of thousands more impoverished emigrants heading for Quebec. With a mounting sense of urgency, Douglas petitioned the authorities for more money to build a new fever hospital, but it was too late. Before new buildings could be erected the little island was overwhelmed. Within a week of the arrival of the *Syria* another 25 vessels arrived with cases of fever and dysentery on board. By early June there were 40 ships laden with 14 000 immigrants at anchor in the St Lawrence. Mortality on some of these vessels had already been appalling. The *Avon* lost 246 passengers out of 552, the *Larch* lost 108 at sea with another 150 people suffering from fever in the hold. Over a thousand of the worst cases were landed on the island while the remaining thousands festered on board the anchored vessels. Many of the ships had run out of food and water. The rotting filth on the passenger decks sent clouds of stinking vapour into the air. Douglas ordered the captains to wash down the decks and open the ports to improve the ventilation, but as long as the passengers remained on board the ships could not be properly cleansed. It was said that the smell of death and decay befouled the air in the little town of Montmagny, more than five miles away.

On the island conditions deteriorated from bad to appalling. Douglas himself fell ill as he struggled to cope with the sick and dying. An observer described him as 'worn out trying to do impossibilities'. There was no deep water quay and sick men, women and children had to be rowed ashore in small boats. Once there, they lay in hurriedly erected sheds, in tents sent down by the army, even on the open ground. Some of the sheds were fitted with tiers of bunks like those on board the ships, and people were loaded on to them, two or three to each space, without regard to age or sex, the lightly-infected side by side with the dead and dying. In some cases patients with chronic diarrhoea lay on the upper bunks with others, too weak to move, beneath them. There were not enough latrines, even for those strong enough to reach them, and the scrub around the tents and sheds was soon foul with human excrement. There was a shortage of food, of clean water, of medicine, most of all a shortage of trained medical assistants.

In all, twenty-two doctors volunteered to help Douglas, but many of them, like Douglas himself, were incapacitated by illness for at least part of the time and before the summer was out, four of them had died. Many of the local clergy, both Roman Catholic and Protestant, also offered assistance, and nearly half of them also died. Many of the most dreadful jobs, particularly burials, were carried out by the army, but soldiers could not be expected to give bedside care and trained nurses were not to be found at any price. Quarantine regulations called for the healthy immigrants to be separated from the sick, but many of the so-called healthy were also infected, and there were nowhere near enough people to care for those who could not help themselves. Some of the passengers who did volunteer had the worst of motives. They robbed the dead and dying. In the sweltering heat of the Canadian summer, many patients lay for hours in their own filth, moaning for water, the living side by side with the dead.

No one knows exactly how many people died on Grosse Ile during the terrible summer of 1847, but Douglas himself spoke of 50 deaths a day at the height of the epidemic and recorded a total of 5424 as being buried on the island. There are many who think this an under-estimate. Nearly 100 000 Irish emigrants left for British North America in the course of the year, three-quarters of them destined for Quebec. Many hundreds, perhaps thousands, died on board the ships before they ever reached Canada and their bodies were dropped overboard. When they died on Grosse Ile, there was neither the time nor the manpower for proper burial and the corpses were placed in mass graves, great trenches cut into the earth and rock, with the rubble piled back on top of the heaps of bodies. One contemporary described the dead as being 'piled up like cordwood'. In the circumstances, it is difficult to imagine that anyone was stopping to count each individual corpse.

One of the ironies of the quarantine system is that the appallingly over-crowded living quarters on Grosse Ile, and the 'fever sheds' of cities such as

Montreal, like the ships on the Atlantic run, provided ideal conditions for typhus to flourish. There are many records of patients recovering and then being re-infected (though the picture is confused by relapsing fever, in which such apparent recoveries are part of the course of the disease). Many patients were discharged if they appeared to be healthy and were given free passage on the river boats into the interior. In the crowded boats, their clothing still infested with lice, they carried infection with them as they travelled up the St Lawrence.

Some ships from Ireland, with no apparent sickness on board, managed to avoid quarantine altogether. By the time the passengers developed fever they were often far inland. There was a serious epidemic of typhus in Montreal, where 7000 people died, and smaller outbreaks in many communities, large and small, as far as Toronto and beyond. As the fever spread to the local population, people blamed the Irish as the source of the infection. Before long, all doors were closed to the new immigrants as they walked the long lonely roads of the Canadian wilderness. In the bitter winter, many died of hunger and cold as surely as they would have done in Ireland. Some authorities believe that as many as 20 000, one in five of the Irish emigrants to Canada in 1847, died before they could complete their journey.

Looking back on 1847, Dr Douglas tried to establish what exactly had caused the terrible mortality. He noted that there was little connection between conditions on board and the prevalence of fever. Many German immigrants had arrived in vessels even more overcrowded than those carrying the Irish passengers, with little or no sickness on board. Nor was it simply a matter of malnutrition. Typhus kills the well-fed just as quickly as it does the undernourished, often quicker because poor people develop some immunity from early exposure to the disease. Other studies have shown that there were some ships where food was in short supply and the passengers were very close to starvation, but there was no fever. The people arrived very thin, but otherwise in good health. Douglas did not have the advantage of knowing the real causes of infection, but he did establish the link between those ports of departure like Liverpool, Cork and Sligo, where fever was rife, and the number of deaths on board the ships.

There was another, rather touching postscript to the Grosse Ile story. Children die all too quickly from dehydration as a consequence of dysentery and there were many such childhood deaths, both on the ships and in the quarantine station. They do not, however, succumb as easily as adults to typhus. The result was that the convents and orphanages of Quebec quickly filled up with children of various ages, both of whose parents had perished from fever. One of these institutions was run by a group of ladies who called themselves 'La Société Charitable des Dames Catholiques de Quebec'. They kept meticulous records of each child in their care, including many Irish children from the emigrant ships. These records show that some of those children were adopted by French-Canadian foster parents, who often allowed them to keep their own names. To this day there are Regans and Sheehans in Quebec who speak no other language than French.

Saint John, New Brunswick, was the other main port of entry to British North America in that terrible year. Moses Perley, the Chief Emigration officer for New Brunswick, was a man of exceptional energy and intelligence and an enthusiastic apostle of mass immigration. During the early 1840s he repeatedly urged the provincial government to build roads and railways to open up the interior, because he believed that the future prosperity of New Brunswick depended on a vastly increased population to exploit the abundant land and natural resources of the country. On the other hand, he also knew that the Irish famine might result in the export, not only of people, but of epidemics of disease. Like his colleagues on Grosse Ile, he saw disaster coming and did his best to prepare for it. He wanted in particular to repair and enlarge the buildings on the quarantine station, a scrap of earth and rock called Partridge Island, which guards the entrance to the harbour at Saint John. Again, like Dr Douglas, Perley was thwarted by official parsimony and short-sightedness. The facilities on Partridge Island, like those on Grosse Ile, were quite inadequate for the huge numbers of sick and impoverished immigrants who landed there in 1847.

In his report on the 1847 disaster, Perley gave a total of 17 074 passengers embarked for New Brunswick on 106 vessels, seven out of Liverpool, the remainder from Irish ports. He estimated the number of emigrants who died within his jurisdiction at 2400, 'or one seventh of those who embarked'.

Like most of his contemporaries, Perley believed that 'ship fever' was caused by overcrowding and poor ventilation on the passenger decks of the emigrant ships. He was highly critical of British masters and ship owners who failed to conform to the regulations laid down by the Passenger Acts and he detained and prosecuted several captains for breaking the law. What angered him most, however, was not the condition of the ships. It was the perception, widely shared in Canada, that the British government and the Irish landlords were simply off-loading the problem of maintaining the Irish poor by dumping them on Canada. He singled out for the sharpest criticism those landlords who had paid passage for poor tenants:

> … to relieve the estates of the expense of their support. They landed in New Brunswick in the greatest misery and destitution, so broken down and emaciated by starvation, disease, and the fatigues of the voyage, as to be in great measure incapable of performing sufficient labour to earn a subsistence.

Several things are plain from the reports of Perley and his contemporaries. Officials were fearful of a fever epidemic. They resented having to meet the cost of providing food, clothing and shelter to thousands of immigrant paupers, but they might have found the cost of doing so less of a burden if they had any hope that the immigrants would one day make a contribution to the wealth and success of their province. Small children, they knew, would have to be maintained on charity for many years. The older immigrants were not only incapable of providing for the very young, but would also be a burden on the community themselves for the rest of their lives. In the event, this burden was somewhat exaggerated. Only 7000 out of the 100 000 Irish immigrants in British North America received any assistance from the state. Despite their difficulties, most of the people somehow managed to provide for themselves.

At the same time, there is evidence that many of the immigrants longed to return to Ireland. Some wrote home, declaring that they would never have made the crossing if they had realized how bad conditions would be on the other side of the Atlantic, and there are several references in New Brunswick papers to Irish beggars going from door to door, pleading for money to enable them to buy their passages back home.

In November, the ship *Aeolus* arrived at Saint John with 428 passengers, almost all from Lord Palmerston's estates in Sligo. Perley made his report:

There are many aged persons of both sexes on board and a large proportion of women and children, the whole in the most abject state of destitution, with barely sufficient rags upon their persons to cover their nakedness ... one boy, about ten years of age, was actually brought on deck stark naked.

Eight passengers died shortly after their arrival. In his meticulous fashion, Perley listed 176 women and 140 children under the age of 14 among the survivors on board. 'The women and children,' he continued, 'were the most helpless and destitute of any who have landed at this port in the last five years.'

It was the second voyage which the *Aeolus* had made that year, and on both occasions she had been carrying tenants whose passages had been paid by their landlords – Lord Palmerston, the famous statesman, and Sir Robert Gore-Booth, his neighbour in County Sligo. The people of Saint John had had

Lord Palmerston. Emigrants from his estate in Ireland were in a wretched condition when they arrived on board the Aeolus *at Saint John, New Brunswick.*

enough. The council passed a resolution stating that all the almshouses and specially requisitioned buildings in the town were full to overflowing and that it was 'totally unable to suggest measures by which this grievously overburdened community can shelter and support such an unheard of mass of misery, thus thrown upon our shores at such an inclement season of the year'. It went on to criticize Lord Palmerston for dumping his tenants on Saint John and made sure that its criticisms were passed on to the Lieutenant Governor. It also recommended that the passengers on the *Aeolus* should be offered a free return passage to Ireland, with sufficient food and water to make certain they would survive the voyage.

The scandal was reported in the British press and Lord Palmerston was eventually obliged to make a statement in the Commons. He claimed that all the arrangements had been conducted by his agents, Kincaid and Stewart, and referred the House to their letter of explanation. Far from sounding repentant, the agents maintained that the emigrants had begged them for a passage, that they had been well supplied with food and clothing, and that the 'exigencies of the voyage' must have been the cause of the sorry state in which they arrived at Saint John.

It is difficult to believe everything the agents wrote, but it is true that Palmerston's estate workers had been provided with food and clothing for the voyage. It is not pleasant to speculate, but it is possible that the nakedness of some of the children was connected with outbreaks of dysentery on board ship. Messrs Kincaid and Stewart's assertions were also given some credibility by a letter which the passengers themselves wrote to the local newspaper in Saint John, acknowledging their debt to Lord Palmerston and thanking the captain of the *Aeolus* for his generosity and kindness. A similar letter was sent to Sir Robert Gore-Booth at his home in County Sligo. It is difficult to know what inducements may have been offered to extract letters of this kind, but within a year of their arrival in New Brunswick, Lord Palmerston's former tenants from the *Aeolus* remitted a total of two thousand pounds to their relatives at home. Perhaps the condition of some of the passengers was not quite as wretched as Perley made out in his report. Like all observers, then and now, Perley had his own agenda for indignation and landlord-assisted emigration was high on his list.

The proposal to repatriate immigrants was quietly dropped. Even if it had not been, it is by no means certain that any of the new immigrants would willingly have returned. Bad though their circumstances might have been, the poor Irish knew that the fate awaiting them at home, however much they might long to return, was no better than the misery they now had to face. A few already had families or friends living in New Brunswick and were eventually able to join them. Others found work in the lumber trade, or joined the construction gangs working on the railroads. Many, especially the old and the frail, stayed close to where they had landed in Saint John. The dockside district of York Point quickly degenerated into a slum, where the poorest immigrants survived as best they could, working at the most menial jobs available and begging from their wealthier neighbours.

A great number of them had never intended to stay in British North America. The United States was the promised land, blessed with unimaginable riches, free of British rule and free of the rigid bounds of class and status which so circumscribed life in nineteenth-century Ireland. Those with the energy and strength to do so often took the first opportunity to travel up the Saint John River to the point where it bordered with the USA. They then faced a long, arduous slog, almost certainly on foot, through Maine and New Hampshire, where they were no more welcome than they were in Canada.

The journey must have been appallingly difficult, especially for families with young children, and many died on the way. So, despite the higher fares, the tendency was for Irish emigrants to take the quicker and easier route, by sailing direct to America. Even in the panic year of 1847 there were nearly 120 000 emigrants to the USA as against less than 100 000 to Canada. In the following year the Canadian authorities introduced more stringent immigration requirements and the difference was far more marked, with 156 000 travelling to the USA as against 23 000 to Canada. The trend continued throughout the famine years with more and more ships sailing direct to American ports. The peak period of famine emigration to Canada began and ended in 1847. For the United States, it had only just begun.

CHAPTER SEVEN

The AMERICAN CONNECTION

*O*n 14 November 1847 a young Irish farmer, his wife and three children set out from New Ross in County Wexford, bound for Boston. The emigrant's name was Patrick Kennedy and one of his many great-grandsons was to become the first Catholic Irish-American to be elected President of the United States of America, John Fitzgerald Kennedy.

The massive Irish emigration to the United States was without doubt the single most important consequence of the famine. Although the exodus had begun earlier in the century, there was an enormous increase in the sheer number of people desperate to escape from Ireland and willing to risk their lives and their futures in the United States. In 1843 just 23 000 made the one-way voyage across the Atlantic. By 1846 numbers had trebled and they continued to increase throughout the famine, reaching a climax in 1851 with a startling total of 219 000 people in just one year.

Emigrants, by definition, were people who could somehow find enough money to pay the passage, very often both for themselves and their families. In 1847 the fare for a whole family might well have been £20, which was four years' wages for a labouring man. Even so, they may well have exhausted all their savings or borrowed heavily from friends and family to take this one desperate

---

John Fitzgerald Kennedy was the great-grandson of a famine immigrant. When he was elected President, many Catholic Irish-Americans realized that their long struggle for full acceptance into United States society was finally at an end.

gamble. By American standards the great majority were poor when they started and poorer still on arrival. The manifests of ships sailing for New York in 1846 show that twenty-five per cent were classified as farmers or artisans, with a small scattering of professional people. The rest were described as labourers or servants. A significant proportion of the better-off were certainly Protestants, which meant that the mass of poorer people landing in the United States, just as in Ireland itself, were Roman Catholics.

While the middle-class Irish often coped very well with their new sur-roundings and were quickly assimilated into American society, the poor were not. Unlike those from other European countries, who were often attracted to virgin farmland on the frontier, the great mass of Irish immigrants headed straight for the big cities on the Atlantic seaboard, for New York, Boston or Philadelphia, and stayed there. The slums of these cities, squalid and over-crowded though they were, proved more attractive to poor Irish people than the open spaces of the west.

Pioneers were reckoned to need about forty pounds to buy, clear and stock a farm on virgin land, and to see them through the first year. Very few Irish immigrants had that kind of money. Many spoke little English and most were not farmers in the fullest sense, but labourers, accustomed only to tilling a tiny plot with spade and hoe. They had few skills which could be adapted to the new environment and their cabins at home, however miserable they may have been, were always close to their neighbours. It must have seemed more companionable, more secure, to stay close to other Irish people in this strange and often hostile country. It may also have been true, though it cannot have seemed so, that there was more opportunity for unskilled labourers and their womenfolk in an urban slum than in the backwoods of the frontier states. The result was that the immigrants went from poverty and hunger in rural Ireland to poverty and hunger in urban America.

The new arrivals in all the American ports were generally in better health than those who arrived in Canada and, despite the sufferings described in 'coffin ship' stories, very few of them died on the voyage. It is often remarked that American ships were better than British ships and that their captains paid more attention to the welfare of passengers. This may well have been true, but very few American ships were employed in the passenger trade during the early years of the famine, so this has little to do with the matter. It may be that immigrants to the United States were marginally better off and had therefore escaped the worst ravages of hunger and disease, and it is certainly true that the US Passenger Acts were stricter and greater attention was paid to the health of those boarding ship in the first place. Some American cities also tried to make sure that no sick Irish people would even set foot on their quays. In 1847, the city of Boston passed a law insisting that the captains of immigrant vessels post a bond of two-thousand dollars for every sick immigrant arriving at the port, but some ships which sailed early in the season did not know of the requirement before their departure and all their passengers held tickets for Boston.

On 17 May 1847, the British brig *Mary*, out of Cork, tried to land forty-six steerage passengers at Boston. The port authorities refused to accept them without the necessary bonds and the captain, a man named Wyman, was unable to comply. He decided to take the ship up to Halifax, Nova Scotia, instead. The *Boston Liberator* reported what happened next:

> The passengers were much exasperated at the turn matters were taking, and when the pilot ordered the crew to weigh anchor, the passengers took possession of the handspikes and windlass, and assaulted Captain Wyman, who called to his assistance Captain Josias Sturgis of the [US] revenue cutter *Hamilton*, when a boat's crew, armed with cutlasses, came on board. Captain Sturgis ordered the women and children to go aft and the men to fall back from the windlass, which they did. He then got the brig under weigh and accompanied her for some distance under a fair and fresh breeze. The resistance of the unfortunate passengers is not to be wondered at, when it is considered that they were not landed at the termination of the voyage, but forced to go on in an entirely different direction from that which they contemplated.

Several other vessels followed the same path, most of them diverting north to Quebec. The extended voyage ensured an even greater number of deaths on board these ships and meant that the survivors became casualties of the

Canadian rather than the US quarantine stations. Nevertheless, a significant number of immigrants did succeed in making it to Boston, either by taking a steamer down from Saint John, New Brunswick, or by trekking overland. The city authorities were obliged to establish a quarantine station and admit several thousand bondless Irish immigrants into the port. Once there, they were virtually confined to one area, known as Ward 8. It had once been a residential district for prosperous Boston citizens, but they had departed for the suburbs, leaving their crumbling mansions behind them. The Irish immigrants were unable to follow them, because the city was divided by waterways and each of the bridges demanded a toll. It was only about twenty cents, but for poor immigrants that was more than enough. They stayed put. The fine old houses were sub-divided into tenements, with crazy wooden annexes to front and rear, and the whole area quickly degenerated into a slum. It was many years before they would be able to leave Ward 8.

But it was New York which took by far the greatest numbers of Irish immigrants in 1847, just as she was to do for many years to come. At the time, New York's quarantine station was on Staten Island, only about four miles from Manhattan. As an isolation centre it was far from ideal, because the island was already a residential area for city workers and there were regular ferries to and from Manhattan. The authorities complained that it was impossible to prevent earlier immigrants to New York from crossing over to the island to visit their sick friends and relatives. The inevitable result was a fever epidemic, which killed 2000 people in the city in the summer of 1847. Fortunately, although conditions were bad on Staten Island, they never approached the horrors of Grosse Ile, and the majority of the Irish arriving in the city landed at the quays on South Street, Manhattan.

As soon as they reached New York, the new arrivals were greeted by 'runners', most of them also Irish and, if possible, even more villainous than those who plagued the quays of Liverpool. The runners would introduce the hapless newcomers to the proprietors of tenement buildings, who frequently robbed them of their possessions and charged them extortionate rents for vile lodgings. Others fell into the hands of 'bondsmen' – lodging house keepers who ran a corrupt racket as middlemen between the shipping firms and the city authorities.

The South Street quay in New York, the point of entry for Irish immigrants at the time of the famine.

New York, like the other American ports, demanded a bond to ensure that sick immigrants were not a burden on the city's poor rates. The bondsmen undertook this obligation, bribed the inspecting officials and fleeced the sick immigrants whom they took into their houses. Most of the bondsmen, like the runners and the tenement keepers, were Irish. The new immigrants had entered the world of cut-throat capitalism at its worst. Many of them, demoralized and disorientated by the sufferings they had endured, sank into a state which was in many respects worse than the horrors they had left behind, because it was a moral as well as a physical collapse.

Whatever their sufferings, and despite the excesses of a few, most poor people in Ireland were law-abiding and honest. They were also renowned for their chastity. In their new home the reverse seems to have been true. For many years after the famine, criminal statistics in New York were dominated by the Irish. Irishmen were notorious for drinking, for brawling, and as the most likely candidates for the prison or the lunatic asylum. In 1857, ten years after the first flood of new immigrants, the Irish tenements in New York still had such a foul reputation that they were made the subject of a special report by a select committee of the House of Assembly.

The members of the committee were motivated by what they themselves called 'political philanthropy' – a combination of genuine compassion and fear that what they perceived as low standards of morality might somehow pollute the purer streams of decent Protestant America. They deplored the prevalence of prostitution, incest and drunkenness among the Irish poor and they gave detailed accounts of the evidence which they found, linking vicious habits with living conditions which 'far exceeded the limit of previously conceived ideas of human degradation and suffering'.

The report went into great detail about living conditions in the 'tenant-houses'. Just as in Boston, the spacious rooms of old New York houses were sub-divided into tiny compartments and, in the yards behind the old mansions, landlords ran up gimcrack wooden tenements, connected to the outside world by a single narrow alley. The people literally scraped a living by gathering horse manure in the streets. The rooms where they lived were tiny, ill-lit, and always crowded. The occupants often had to make do without a stick of furniture and were reduced to cooking their meagre meals on crude charcoal braziers. These wretched buildings were a permanent fire hazard, dirty, and profoundly insanitary. There was rarely any provision for clean water and such latrines as were available were totally inadequate for the numbers of people who had to use them. The only amenity which even the most ramshackle tenements provided was a 'grocer's', where cheap provisions and cheaper corn whiskey were freely available, even to children. In the view of the committee, conditions were made even worse by the neglect of the landlords and the:

> … reckless slovenliness, discontent, privation and ignorance among the tenants [which] were left to work out their invariable result in the destruction of doors, shutters, windows, fences, ceilings, floors, until the entire premises reached the level of tenant house dilapidation, containing, but sheltering not, the miserable hordes that crowded beneath mouldering, water-rotted roofs, or burrowed among the rats in clammy cellars … We could tell of one room, twelve feet by twelve, in which were five resident families, comprising twenty persons of both sexes and all ages, with only two beds, without partition or screen, or chair or table; and all dependent for their support upon the sale of chips gleaned from the street at four cents a basket.

As if the living conditions were not bad enough, tenants were evicted for non-payment of rent even more swiftly and with far less prevarication than they would have been in Ireland. Even in famine conditions, all Irish landlords had to go through a legal process, however cursory it might be, before attempting to evict tenants. In New York that was not necessary. The landlord had his bully boys on hand to make sure there was no trouble. If the rent was not paid every week the tenants were thrown into the street, even in the bitter cold of a New York winter. So it is probably true, as one immigrant claimed, that the life expectancy of most Irish people in their new home was less than five years.

Not all the tenants in this wretched situation were Irish. The committee observed that some neighbourhoods were occupied by poor Germans, who soon moved on to better areas. Other slum tenements were crowded with African-Americans, some of the men married to Irish women, but relations between the

Irish and their black neighbours were generally poor. Both ethnic groups were subject to prejudice and discrimination. Both groups had also suffered the effects of social breakdown. Tight-knit traditional Irish communities, with a long tradition of mutual aid and a strong sense of morality had been shattered by the combined effects of famine and emigration, just as African communities had been destroyed by slavery. Some individuals in both groups were no doubt as morally upright as they had ever been, but social cohesion had gone; for most, it was survival that mattered. Freed slaves and immigrant Irish battled in the gutter to avoid being relegated to the bottom of the heap.

Even for those with energy and determination, it was difficult to escape from the slums. The Irish, whether deservedly or not, had a bad reputation for drunkenness and unreliability. They also faced religious discrimination from Protestant employers. New Yorkers from an earlier, largely Anglo-Saxon, generation of settlers, regarded them with suspicion and resentment. They may have turned out the British, but that did not mean that they welcomed poor Irish Catholics, who might settle for lower wages and depress their standards of living. Extremists, calling themselves 'Nativists', or 'Know Nothings', campaigned against the Irish in the press, subjecting them to caricatures every bit as vile as those in the British papers. They tried to get them sent back to Ireland and did their utmost to exclude them from employment. The words 'No Irish need apply' were commonly attached to advertisements for jobs or accommodation.

Despite all these disadvantages, the Irish gradually pulled themselves out of the ghettos. Sheer numbers played a part in this. In 1845 the population of New York was 350 000. By 1850 it was over 500 000 with the Irish making up the bulk of the increase. By this time there were over a million Irish-born people in the United States, most of them living in the centres of big cities. No democratic country can afford to ignore the claims of such a formidable number of potential voters. The US economy, despite periodic slumps and depressions, was also expanding at a tremendous rate and there was a growing

Irish 'tenant houses' in New York were centres of crime, poverty and disease for decades after the first wave of famine immigration.

demand for labour in the construction industry. Despite discrimination, most Irish people eventually found work, the men usually as unskilled labourers, the women often in domestic service. Another factor which helped them was the skill which many men had acquired back in Ireland at forming themselves into 'combinations' and secret societies to resist the demands of landlords and agents. In the infant trade unions, in local city politics, and, as time went by, in the Democratic Party, Irish-Americans eventually emerged as a powerful force.

The role of the Church, from a secular point of view, was more equivocal. On the one hand Catholicism provided those poor immigrants who still clung to their faith with spiritual support and a sense of collective identity. Priests exhorted their congregations to acquire the Yankee virtues of industry and sobriety and no doubt they had some influence. On the other hand, Catholicism delayed full assimilation into the mainstream of nineteenth-century American life, with its Protestant majority and lively suspicion of 'Romish' practices. Irish Protestants, with a religious and cultural background far closer to that of most Americans, were far more easily absorbed. But they also resented the arrival of hordes of their Catholic fellow-countrymen and there were Orange versus Green riots in most American cities during the middle years of the nineteenth century. Catholicism remained a focus for hostility and a bar to advancement in many professions for almost a century.

The difficulties experienced by the Catholic Irish in their new surroundings were reflected in their dual allegiance. They were committed to the United States, even though many Americans rejected them, but they pined for Ireland. People who had fought and struggled for a place on an emigrant ship, and there were many of them, were often so bruised by their experiences in their new country that they began to feel increasingly bitter about their exile. Even those who did well, and their numbers increased as the years went by, shared this mixture of nostalgia for home and anger that they could not have achieved the same success in Ireland. Once they might have seen the famine and their own mass exodus as a terrible but unavoidable calamity, an Act of God. As time went by, more and more came to see it as the act of the British Government. If they were slow to see it that way, there were those who were keen to educate them.

After the fiasco of the 1848 rising, many of the leaders of the Young Ireland movement fled the country to avoid arrest and made their way to the United

Irish Catholics in the United States faced vicious discrimination
from earlier Protestant immigrants. One result of this was a
series of Orange versus Green riots which erupted from time to
time in every major city on the eastern seaboard.

States, the one country where they were sure of being able to escape British
retribution and find a sympathetic hearing from their own countrymen. Others,
like John Mitchel and Thomas Meagher, had been sentenced to transportation,
but later escaped from Tasmania and eventually arrived in New York. James
Stephens, John O'Mahony, Michael Doheny and several others were also in the
city. None of these men had any interest in becoming Americans. They were
Irish nationalists, fiercely determined to win freedom for their country. In New
York, the group launched its own newspapers and set about propagating the
nationalist cause among the immigrant population.

It was very successful. The Young Irelanders themselves had been quite
literally forced into emigration by the British government and they found it easy

to persuade others that they had all shared a common fate and a common enemy. The most prolific and effective writer among them was John Mitchel. Mitchel rightly attacked the monstrous brutalities of past generations of British conquerors, the terrible injustice of Irish land tenure under British rule and the blind adherence to 'political economy' of the British government during the famine, but he went much further than that. He portrayed British policy as a deliberate conspiracy to reduce the Irish to submission by starving millions of them to death or forcing them to emigrate – 'America or the grave', as he put it.

Mitchel was a master of the vivid phrase and the judicious exaggeration. In writing of Peel's imports of maize, for example, he said that 'a Government ship, sailing into any harbour with Indian corn, was sure to meet half a dozen sailing out with Irish wheat and cattle'. Though of Presbyterian upbringing himself, he also knew just how to play to the Catholic majority. Many of his phrases became popular currency and are still quoted as fact by Irish-Americans today. Mitchel's famous summary of the famine was to become an article of faith:

> Now those 1 500 000 men, women and children, were carefully, prudently and peacefully *slain* by the English Government. They died of hunger, in the midst of abundance, which their own hands created; and it is quite immaterial to distinguish between those who perished in the agonies of famine itself from those who died from typhus fever, which in Ireland is always caused by famine.
>
> Further, this was strictly an *artificial* famine – that is to say, it was a famine which desolated a rich and fertile island, that produced every year abundance and super-abundance to sustain all her people and many more. The English indeed, call that famine a dispensation of Providence; and ascribe it entirely to the blight of the potatoes. But potatoes failed in like manner all over Europe, yet there was no famine save in Ireland. The British account of the matter, then, is, first a fraud; second a blasphemy. The Almighty, indeed, sent the potato blight, but the English created the famine.

There are all kinds of quibbles which can be raised over these words, with their extravagant overstatement and economy with the truth. No matter.

Mitchel was not aiming at a highly educated audience, but at a partisan reader-ship, eager to believe what he had to tell them. His words made perfect sense to people who had seen British soldiers escorting convoys of food through crowds of starving people, or a British officer standing by while the bailiff's men cleared a village of its wretched occupants. There was enough truth in what Mitchel wrote for his words to carry conviction. They convinced thousands.

Mitchel went on to an unsavoury career as a newspaper editor, defending the slavery of Blacks on American plantations and opposing the emancipation of Jews. His nationalism and his passionate longing for liberty were strictly for the Irish. But he was enormously effective. By portraying the British as the deliber-ate architects of genocide and exile, he provided Irish immigrants with a target for their anger. Other Americans were treating them badly, exploiting them, denying them advancement, but anger with the United States would have been counter-productive. By blaming the British for all their troubles, Mitchel also gave his Irish readers absolution for any failures or sins on their own account. In the place of remorse, or inchoate misery, he gave them hatred.

The liberating atmosphere of the United States, despite the ugly squalor of its slums, also gave the Irish immigrants a sense of empowerment. They began to see that political freedom could be achieved and that shaking off the burden of colonialism was a goal worth striving for. They had escaped from the world of poor rates, of workhouses, of a class-bound social system that demanded craven obedience to the landlord, at least to his face. There was a certain nobility in the demand for freedom from British oppression, and many of the new Irish-Americans were able to see this more clearly from a distance than had been possible at home in Ireland.

Besides Mitchel, there were other politically-active Young Irelanders in the United States, who were just as passionate in their nationalism and more direct in their methods. In 1858, John O'Mahony and Michael Doheny in New York linked up with James Stephens, who had returned to Ireland to form a new and secret organization, dedicated to the liberation of their homeland. Stephens' Irish-based group had no name to begin with, but it was later to mature into an organization which would play a great part in the evolution of an independent Ireland, the Irish Republican Brotherhood, or IRB. O'Mahony, more romantic, called the American arm the Fenian Brotherhood – which was said to be an allusion to the army of the legendary hero Fiann McCool. The name captured the Irish imagination; before long, all more or less secret Irish nationalist groups were known, by friend and foe alike, as Fenians.

The Fenians might possibly have gone the same way as many other paramilitary groups, which flowered briefly in the United States in the years following the famine, if it had not been for the Civil War. Although Irishmen had a long and distinguished record as volunteers in other peoples' armies, they did not take kindly to conscription. In 1863, when they felt that the draft boards for the Union Army were unfairly singling out too high a proportion of Irishmen, they rioted, lynching four black men, looting, burning, and fighting a pitched battle with the militia.

Nevertheless, thousands of Irishmen volunteered for military service and Irish units fought courageously and successfully in the Union armies. One Irish regiment, the 69th, won particular distinction at the first battle of Bull Run. Second-in-command of the regiment in this action was Thomas Meagher, a former member of 'Young Ireland'. He went on to become a Brigadier General in the Union Army and commanding officer of the Irish Brigade. After several brilliant actions, he led a hopeless assault on Marye's Heights at Fredericksburg. The brigade was shattered, but its courage won the admiration of the Confederate commander, Robert E. Lee. 'Never were men so brave,' he wrote. 'They ennobled their race by their splendid gallantry on that desperate occasion.'

The glory which Irish regiments won during the Civil War helped them to win self-confidence and to gain the respect of their fellow Americans, but military encampments also made an ideal recruiting ground for political movements. Young men, many of whom had come over to the United States as children during the famine years, were ready converts to the Fenian cause and the organization mushroomed with astonishing speed. The result was that by the war's end there were up to 1000 potential volunteers for an army of liberation, trained, battle-hardened, and with easy access to arms.

The Fenian leaders vacillated over how and when to launch an attack on the British. Two rather misguided attempts were made to invade Canada, which met with little success. The problems of launching a war of liberation in Ireland itself were formidable. The leaders knew that their lines of communication across the Atlantic were long and hazardous and that a campaign, once

Irish soldiers in the Union Army. Their courage in the Civil War
helped Irish-Americans gain acceptance in Yankee society.

launched, would be difficult to supply and re-inforce. What the Fenians needed was for Britain to be distracted by some foreign crisis, or for Americans to be drawn into the conflict, but the United States was mending its wounds after a cruel civil war and the British Army was not at that time involved in any major operation abroad.

Fenian emissaries, sent to assess the situation in Ireland, were easily tracked by the British authorities, and the cells which they set up were speedily infiltrated by government spies. Reports about their activities appeared regularly in the newspapers and the authorities had plenty of time to send for reinforcements and prepare for trouble. Church leaders preached against Fenianism, as they always did against secret, revolutionary organizations, and the rebels had little public support.

The Fenians called for a countrywide insurrection in February. At the last moment they called it off, but a messenger sent to Kerry failed to reach the rebels there before the appointed hour. The Kerry men rebelled on their own and were swiftly crushed. The leaders finally launched their insurrection on the night of 6 March 1867. The operation was badly co-ordinated and badly led. The Fenians had planned simultaneous risings all over the country, but they lacked sufficient trained soldiers and the majority of the insurgents were wretchedly armed and totally unprepared for battle. Like other Irish rebels before them, they also suffered ill luck. A group of Fenian officers were captured before they could even reach their commands and many of the volunteers were left leaderless.

Even so, it was a curious rebellion. In Dublin itself it was a shambles. On the night of 6 March, a night of high wind and driving snow, large parties of young men were spotted by the constabulary, heading out of the city and towards the suburbs. They had gathered at various pubs in the city, where they had been given bread and meat and perhaps a little Dutch courage and had then been directed to assembly points in the outer suburbs. Some of these groups were armed. Others were accompanied by cartloads of pikes, antique muskets and 'American swords' covered in straw. A small crowd of about forty were intercepted by three policemen on the road to Tallaght, several miles from the city centre. There was a scuffle, the leader was stabbed with a police bayonet and the rest ran off.

The Dublin *News Letter* carried a full report the following morning:

Last night at ten o'clock, about five hundred Fenians collected at Temple Road, Rathmines … and afterwards joined a similar number at Tallaght, seven miles from Dublin. They were provisioned with bread and meat, and armed with rifles, revolvers, daggers, knives, and American swords. Many were mere youths.

A large military force, under Lord Strathnairn, consisting of detachments of 9th Lancers and 52nd Regiment, are driving them to the mountains.

A body of 150 were met by a party of fourteen police. The latter called upon them to surrender. but the Fenians fired, and the police returned it, wounding five, two mortally. None of the police were injured. About 150 prisoners were taken, also six wagon loads of ammunition, captured on Tallaght Hill.

*The Fenian leader, 'Colonel' Kelly, was arrested by the police
and later rescued in a daring raid on the police van taking him
to prison in Manchester.*

It later emerged that the rebels were under orders to avoid confrontation
with Government forces if at all possible. The *News Letter* supported the
Government and may have been partial in its reporting. Were the Fenians
really the first to open fire, or was it the police? We may never know.

It is more than likely that the Fenians' leaders never expected or intended a
military victory. Irish nationalism has often achieved more by martyrdom than
by military success. The nationalist *Nation* newspaper, which had been opposed
to the rising from the first, had some prescient, if slightly florid, comments to
make:

> Between 1172 and 1867 there reaches a long roll of years; nearly seven
> centuries, a great while wherewith to try out any possible experiments

in human affairs. Yet England finds herself today exactly where she was hundreds of years ago, putting down a rebellion in Ireland ... It is a dismal, wild, despairing, mad attempt; as senseless and helpless as the struggle of the captive who dashes to his own destruction against the massive walls and iron bars of his dungeon! It will be easily suppressed. Little of prowess need the British Empire display, little fame has it to win, in crushing a conspiracy and a rebellion such as this. Yet is there something in it most disquieting to England. If but one shot was fired, but one life lost in the present struggle, though the shout of insurrection was heard but for an hour on the Irish hills, another stroke has been dealt at the basis of her moral position here.

When the rebellion had been crushed, the British undermined their moral position still further by pursuing the fleeing rebels with merciless efficiency. The Fenians had very little sympathy from the Irish people before they rebelled, but when the British rounded up the leaders, put them on trial and sentenced them to long terms of imprisonment, public sentiment swung round on the side of the losers. In September 1867 the self-styled Colonel Kelly, one of the principal leaders of the uprising, was arrested in Manchester. His comrades mounted one of those brilliant guerrilla-style ambushes, at which Irish fighters often excelled, and held up the police van carrying him to gaol. Unfortunately, in shooting off the lock to the van, they shot and killed one of the police guards. Four men, Allen, Condon, Larkin, and O'Brien, were subsequently arrested and charged with murder.

They were found guilty and sentenced to death on evidence which was, to say the least, flimsy. It later transpired that Condon was utterly innocent, had been nowhere near the scene of the crime and had a rock-solid alibi. His sentence was quashed, but those of the other three were confirmed. In Ireland, outrage at the way the trial was conducted combined with admiration for the courage of the protagonists to turn Allen, Larkin and O'Brien into popular heroes. Much more recent parallels in modern Anglo-Irish history would not be hard to find, but in those days capital punishment made second thoughts about shaky evidence unproductive. When the three heroes were executed they became martyrs. Foreshadowing the events of 1916, they achieved far more by their deaths than they could have hoped to do alive in arousing popular support for Irish independence, and the 'Manchester Martyrs' remain part of nationalist iconography to this day.

The Fenian uprising and its aftermath also prompted at least one great British statesman to think hard about the Irish cause. William Ewart Gladstone was shocked into awareness of the injustice of British rule in Ireland and the Home Rule movement can be said to have been conceived during that period. At the same time, the failure of the Fenians convinced Irish revolutionaries, especially James Stephens, that they must rely on their own home-grown movement for positive action. From then on, Stephens became increasingly contemptuous of Irish-American activists, but that did not stop him from taking their money, and the connection so established, of Irish-American funding for nationalist activity in Ireland, continued up to the present day. Stephens's organization, the IRB, was destined to outlive him and become the principal force behind the 1916 Easter Rising.

Irish nationalists were not the only people to gain from American money. As soon as they could afford to do so, most new immigrants sent money home and thousands of poor Irish families benefited from the dollars received from absent sons and daughters. A total of 260 million dollars was repatriated by Irish emigrants to the United States in the half century up to 1900. Letters and money combined to attract new waves of emigration and so the transatlantic tide of Irish people continued to flow throughout the second half of the nineteenth century and well into the twentieth. Between 1851 and 1921 another four and a half million Irish people poured into the United States.

Although the great majority of the famine immigrants remained poor, later generations were better equipped and found a more receptive environment awaiting them. In American cities they could attend flourishing Catholic churches with large Irish congregations; they could read Irish newspapers and seek work with city councils dominated by Irish politicians. Some new arrivals went into business and prospered. Many men joined the city service departments, the police, the fire service, while many women, benefiting from the schools provided by the Church, eventually became teachers themselves. Irish people gradually became accepted as respectable American citizens. The prejudice diminished, then slowly disappeared. 'When John F. Kennedy was

The New York police force was one route to respectability for Irish-Americans in the later years of the nineteenth century.

elected President,' says the Irish-American historian, Peter Quinn, 'I knew we'd finally arrived.'

Even among the later generations of immigrants, who knew very well that they had left Ireland willingly, there were many who found their loyalties divided between their new country and the one they had left behind and in the end they often convinced themselves that they too had been driven into exile by the hated British. Irish-Americans continued to lend powerful support to the movement for independence in Ireland. The Ancient Order of Hibernians, which was revived and hugely expanded in America, became a powerful voice for Irish-American distrust of the British. Before the First World War it was an outspoken supporter of Germany in her rivalry with Great Britain. In 1915, a year after the outbreak of war, Irish and German immigrants combined in protest against any possible American involvement in hostilities. Although President Wilson eventually won the day against 'those who insist on a hyphen in their name', Irish-American hostility to Britain was a powerful factor in delaying the United States' entry into the war.

By the time of the Second World War, anti-British sentiment was much more muted. Irish-Americans had become conscious of their strength as respected citizens of the most powerful country in the world. Today, Irish-Americans are perhaps the most successful and certainly one of the most numerous communities in the United States. Forty million Americans are said to count at least one Irish person among their ancestors. Most of them have no particular attachment to their Irish descent, beyond perhaps a willingness to wear the green on St Patrick's Day, but they retain an affection for the old country and they remain sensitive to Irish political issues, especially those where Britain is involved. One measure of this sensitivity was the Clinton administration's willingness to arbitrate in the peace process in Northern Ireland and the ready hearing given to the Sinn Fein leader, Gerry Adams. If asked to explain their sympathy for the nationalist cause, modern Irish-Americans will often mention Britain's terrible treatment of Ireland during the Great Famine, and quote John Mitchel to prove it.

CHAPTER EIGHT

WHO IS TO BLAME?

*I*n the autumn of 1848 the potato crop failed again as completely as it had done in the autumn of 1846. This was the final blow for thousands of cottiers, who starved their families in order to keep enough seed for the crop, somehow found the strength to plant and hoe, and then managed to survive until the potatoes were ready to lift. It was a black and rotten harvest. They now had no alternative but to give up their holdings and go on relief, but relief was no longer obtainable in many of the Poor Law unions. Most landowners and almost all tenants in the most distressed areas had stopped paying rates. The unions no longer had any money with which to pay for supplies and the tradesmen refused to give them credit. They turned to the British Government for help, but no help was forthcoming. The Chancellor, Sir Charles Wood, refused on more than one occasion to send any more money to Ireland.

Following Smith O'Brien's futile rebellion that summer, there was an even more intense hardening of attitudes in England. Even the charities were becoming more cautious. The Society of Friends had given up its soup kitchens and was now concentrating on providing seed and lending money for fisheries and other self-supporting enterprises. The Quakers took the view that the problems were 'far beyond the reach of private exertion. The Government alone could raise the funds and carry out the measures necessary in many districts to save the lives of the people'. Only the British Association kept up a big programme to provide daily meals for schoolchildren throughout the stricken

A million dead.

areas of the west. In 1848 this charity distributed £160 000 in just three months, but the British Government had given up any pretence of generosity. In the first two years of the famine it had spent some eight million pounds on relief, most of this in the form of loans which were eventually written off. However, through-out the almost equally terrible years that followed, it spent less than £500 000.

Such compassion as the Whig ministers may have felt had evidently been exhausted, but reports of continuing starvation and destitution continued to come in from many parts of the country. The details were sometimes horrific. In defence of a case of theft, a resident magistrate gave sworn testimony that the man's wife had gone mad with hunger and had eaten the flesh of her own dead child. In other districts there were reports that the dogs had been eating the dead and starving people were now eating the dogs. But the distress went far beyond individual horror stories. In Ballina, County Mayo, the union was £18 000 in debt and there were 21 000 people on outdoor relief. In Bantry, County Cork, there were 3000 paupers living in the utmost squalor in the work-house. By January 1849 there were 18 000 on outdoor relief in Kilrush, County Clare, and by April there were over 20 000.

Conditions in many workhouses were appalling and the Government's own inspectors sent in report after report, chronicling the shortcomings of the Poor Law system. The following extract is from a letter sent in March 1848 by the newly-appointed vice-guardians about the workhouse in Ennistymon, County Clare:

> We found the dormitories very badly kept, the floors and platforms badly swept, the straw on the beds exceedingly dirty and collections of dirt and filth almost under every bed. On inspecting the laundry, we found the clothes, which had been washed and were in the process of drying, completely covered in vermin, and the persons and clothes of the paupers generally neglected.

In the spring of 1849 the Government finally decided that something must be done, but, once again, the burden of caring for Ireland's poor must be borne by Ireland alone. One of the problems, clearly, was that some of the Poor Law unions were far too large. Ballina, for instance, stretched from the borders

THE ENGLISH LABOURER'S BURDEN;

Or, THE IRISH OLD MAN OF THE MOUNTAIN.

Punch *cartoon of 1849. The British Government refused to advance more than a niggardly £50 000 for famine relief in that year. The English were suffering from an advanced case of 'compassion fatigue' and the Irish poor were caricatured as a burden on the English taxpayer.*

of Sligo to the furthest reaches of Erris, a distance of almost fifty miles, most of it remote moorland and bog. The Poor Law Commission now reorganized some of the more unwieldy unions and increased the total number from 130 to 163.

The Government also recognized, rather late in the day, that there was a fundamental defect in the Poor Law system. Those impoverished districts with the greatest numbers of people in desperate need were also the districts where the rates were the highest and the ratepayers least able to pay. Instead of finding extra money from the Treasury to fund the bankrupt unions, the

Government brought in a measure known as rate-in-aid. Under this scheme, the better-off unions in Ireland were to be made to subsidize the poorest.

This legislation caused great indignation, especially in Ulster, but for once it was not seen as a sectarian issue. The rage of Catholic and Protestant alike was directed at the British Government. Why should prosperous County Down support destitute Mayo, while equally prosperous Lancashire contributed nothing? In a letter to their MP, the Guardians at Newry noted that the whole of Ireland was held to be an integral part of the United Kingdom and, since: 'Ulster has no relations with Connaught which are not equally shared by any other division of the British Empire, we repudiate the separating principle upon which the proposition of the government proceeds'. In fact, the measure made a mockery of the Act of Union, under which Ireland was supposed to be part of Britain. The Government ignored the protests and advanced a parsimonious fifty thousand pounds for immediate needs.

Perhaps to remind Ireland of the true meaning of British sovereignty, the Lord Lieutenant chose this year of 1849 as the occasion for a State Visit by Queen Victoria. 'Arise thee, oh Erin,' went the anthem, composed specially for the occasion, 'look up through thy tears. / The Queen of the Isles in thy cities appears.' It says a great deal for the patience and essential peacefulness of the Irish people that the visit, to Cork, Dublin and Belfast, went off without any violent incident. On the contrary, it was a great success. Her Majesty attended receptions, balls, and firework displays, paid visits to all manner of worthy institutions, and made endless processions in an open carriage through streets full of enthusiastic crowds. There were plenty of opportunities for assassination by gunfire, or by hurling a bomb into the Queen's barouche. Nobody even threw a rotten potato.

In Cork – a day's easy sailing from starving Bantry and Skibbereen – the local fishermen, all neatly dressed in brand new Guernsey frocks and straw hats, presented Her Majesty with a salmon adorned with shamrock. During her visit to Dublin, the Queen was 'cheered with the utmost enthusiasm' by the Roman Catholic students at Maynooth and witnessed 'a genuine Irish jig' danced by prettily-dressed 'peasantry' on the lawns at Carton. In Dublin, she made a speech alluding to the famine in terms which might have been approved by Trevelyan himself:

I gladly share with you the hope that the heavy visitation, with which Providence has recently visited large numbers of my people in this country, is passing away. I have felt deeply for their sufferings, and it will be a source of heartfelt satisfaction to me if I am permitted to witness the future and lasting prosperity of this portion of the United Kingdom.

Before she had finished her speech the Queen was interrupted by a band in the courtyard outside, which jumped its cue and pitched into 'God Save the Queen', so that nobody could hear a word she was saying. With some presence of mind, she ordered the anthem to be stopped, and only resumed speaking when silence had been restored.

Altogether, the visit lasted two weeks and was generally accounted a great success. The *Illustrated London News* enthused:

The mutual satisfaction of the Queen and the people of Ireland towards each other will lead to a still more intimate acquaintance on both sides. Her Majesty's delight at the unexpected cordiality of her Irish people is no secret. She has found her way into their hearts; and we trust that in future years both England and Ireland will see the happy results of the confidence which will date from her first visit.

There is no reason to believe that these sentiments were insincere on either side, even if the words do ring a little hollow in retrospect. The Queen's own diary records her appreciation of the enthusiastic reception she was given by the Irish crowd. She also noticed their ragged and poverty-stricken appearance and was grieved by it. On her return, she sent £200 to the British Association in addition to the £2000 she had already subscribed. It may not have been much, but at least it was more than the £5 note with which she is usually credited in famine mythology.

Meanwhile, Ireland continued to starve. In Kilrush, the 'heavy visitation' which 'Providence' had sent to so many people showed no sign of ending. When the Board of Guardians recovered control of the union in October, it set a much lower rate, but even so the bailiffs failed to collect it. By November there was no money to feed the thousands of paupers on outdoor relief, and even those inside the workhouse had been reduced to a diet of soup and chopped turnips. On 12 December 1849, a Kilrush resident sent a report to the *Limerick and Clare Examiner:*

> The streets of our town are thronged … with swarms of famished, miserable beings, piteously screaming for and craving the least morsel of food. Along the roads that lead to the town may be seen numbers of cars laden with emaciated, half-naked creatures, huddled together in loathsome squalidness, proceeding to the workhouse, where they hope to be relieved; but from whence, alas! after they remain fainting and shivering whole days, and some times nights together, they are obliged to return to their hovels and die in despair …

Contrasting views of events in 1849 from the Illustrated London News. *Below: Captain Kennedy and his six-year-old daughter distributing clothes to the poor in Kilrush. Right: Queen Victoria observing a 'merry jig' at a private house near Dublin.*

The same evening, a ferry carrying just such a load of misery across a local creek capsized and thirty-seven men, women and children were drowned. Two days later, the Chairman of the Board of Guardians, Colonel Vandeleur, was pelted with filth when he unwisely ventured into the streets of Kilrush. Thanks to Captain Kennedy's reports, many of which had been relayed to the House of Commons, the scandal of the evictions on Vandeleur's estate and the desperate state of the union was beginning to claim national attention. A reporter from the *Illustrated London News* visited the town and sent back some vivid sketches. One of them is a sentimental picture of Kennedy's small daughter, doling out clothes to the poor, while her father looked on. It was an image calculated to excite a charitable response in English readers.

The reporter visited other parts of Clare and neighbouring Galway, leaving his readers in no doubt that the misery was widespread. In his account he made

it clear that the landlords were to blame for evicting the poor from their estates, but he also pointed out that the landlords themselves were the victims of 'a vicious system', meaning the Poor Law and all that it implied for ratepayers and their unfortunate tenants. He had a point, but in Kilrush it was difficult for even the most partial onlooker to sympathize with the landlords and richer tenants, who had now succeeded in evicting nearly 20 000 people. The wretched victims either died, thereby saving the ratepayers from additional expense, or joined the hordes of starving paupers, waiting to be fed. Colonel Vandeleur complained to the Poor Law Commissioners that most of the problems were caused by the indiscriminate giving of outdoor relief. Secretly, he also began to work behind the scenes to get rid of Captain Kennedy.

In May 1850 there was a parliamentary enquiry into the affairs of the Kilrush union, which drew on evidence from such a variety of vested interests that it had no hope of arriving at useful conclusions. Kennedy and one of the local parish priests, Father Meehan, were called upon, but so too were Colonel Vandeleur and Marcus Keane. The Kilrush Guardians escaped censure, but they resented the publicity and the light which it had thrown on the evictions in the union. In August they eventually succeeded in persuading the Poor Law Commission to sack Captain Kennedy, who was obliged to pack up and leave. Crowds of people followed him to the quay when he boarded the steamer and the place was said to be in 'deep mourning and grief'. Subsequently, Kennedy took offence at an item in a newspaper report and challenged Vandeleur to a duel. The landlord wisely declined the invitation and sued his challenger for libel. He lost the case, but he did not lose his estate and the evictions continued. In fact Vandeleur's son was still getting rid of surplus tenants in the 1880s.

In the most distressed areas of Ireland the famine lingered on. For lack of any alternative, the poor people who still had access to a plot of land continued to grow potatoes and the potatoes continued to be afflicted by recurrent attacks of blight. (It was not until the 1880s that a French scientist discovered that a mixture of lime and copper sulphate sprayed on the leaves was effective in preventing the disease. During the intervening years, thousands of poor people continued to suffer from periods of starvation as a result of the failure of their staple crop.) Following the mass evictions of the late 1840s there were also many thousands who had no land at all and were obliged to seek refuge in the workhouses, where disease was still rampant. In Kilrush 1700 deaths were registered in the workhouse, mostly of children, between March 1850 and March 1851. How many died outside the workhouse, in the hovels on the hillsides and the ditches of the estates, will never be known. In many other districts starvation and suffering continued, while the British Government lavished money on the Great Exhibition and spent tens of millions on putting down the Indian Mutiny and waging a pointless war in the Crimea. It was no consolation to the Irish, but the Government showed just as little regard for the welfare of British soldiers in the frozen swamps of the Crimea as it had for the starving peasants of Ireland.

By the autumn of 1851 the situation in most parts of Ireland had stabilized, but much had changed. A census taken in that year spelled out the most terrible of those changes, the disappearance of so many people. In 1841 the population had been estimated at a little over eight million. Given the average rate of increase at the time, this meant that Ireland should have had over nine million people by 1851. Instead, there were only six and a half. At first sight, it seemed that the population had fallen by about two and a half million. Most historians now believe that about a million people emigrated and a million people died, which leaves a further half million missing from the record.

The answer to this sad mystery is that birth rates also fell during the famine. In the remote parish of Goleen in west Cork there were 418 Roman Catholic baptisms in 1845 and 62 in 1847. Other parish records in destitute areas show an almost equally dramatic fall in the number of baptisms, even in Church of Ireland registers, albeit on a smaller scale. Some of these 'missing' babies may have been stillbirths or infant deaths, but many thousands of women and girls must have ceased to menstruate and become infertile through malnutrition. It almost goes without saying that the number of marriages also dropped sharply during the famine years and births out of wedlock were rare in Ireland in those days. The resident population would therefore have declined, even without any deaths from starvation or disease. On the other hand, some authorities are convinced that the 1841 census failed to include many of the poorer inhabitants in remote districts. Taking all these ugly variables into account, there can be little doubt that at least a million people died as a direct result of the famine.

In some areas there is evidence that men died in greater numbers than women during the early months of the famine, no doubt because of the hard labour on the Public Works. Overall figures, however, show that famine deaths were mostly in those age bands always most at risk, the elderly and, most of all, the very young. No part of Ireland escaped this dreadful loss, but it was very unevenly distributed. The worst hit county was almost certainly Mayo. Excess deaths, that is the numbers of people who died over and above the normal rate of mortality, have been estimated at between sixty and seventy per cent for Mayo. In the ghastly league table of death, Roscommon, Sligo and Galway were close behind. Leitrim and Cavan also suffered very badly, and so, to a slightly lesser extent, did Clare, Cork, Fermanagh, Monaghan, and so on through the list of thirty-two counties, with none of them escaping unscathed. In the north east, there were pockets of starvation, particularly in hilly areas such as the Mourne mountains in County Down, and, although the wages from the linen industry and vigorous efforts by local charities kept starvation at bay in most of the towns, there were thousands of deaths from typhus and cholera even in Belfast. Wealthy, wheat-growing Carlow and Wexford probably suffered least in terms of the numbers of people who died, but even here there were many who fled the land, never to return.

The pattern of emigration set up during the famine continued, reaching a peak in the 1870s when nearly one-sixth of the total population left the country, most of them bound for the United States. In 1847 many families had crossed the Atlantic as a group, but increasingly, as the years passed, the majority of emigrants were young single people, and this annual haemorrhage continues to the present day. Those who were left behind often remained unmarried, or married later in life and raised smaller families. The decline in population which began with the famine continued. Ironically, this was not so in some of the poorest parts of Connacht, where early marriages and large families remained the rule until quite late in the nineteenth century, but by 1900 the population of the country as a whole had fallen to four million and today, nearly a century later, it is still only five million.

Apart from the disappearance of people from great tracts of land, the most remarkable transformation was in the size of the farms on which people tried to make a living. Prior to the famine, in 1841, about forty-five per cent of all

A rare photograph of Irish tenant farmers and their wives from the mid-nineteenth century. The better off tenant farmers often prospered as a result of the famine.

holdings in Ireland were of less than five acres. By 1851 the proportion had fallen to just over fifteen per cent. Farms of between five and fifteen acres also declined slightly, but those of over fifteen acres showed a substantial increase. The conclusion is clear. The people who held the smallest amount of land – those most utterly dependent on potatoes – were the most vulnerable. By 1851 most of them had either died, or drifted into the towns, or they had emigrated. The people who held larger farms, somewhere between fifteen and thirty acres, did not just survive, they gained by the famine. They took over the vacant smallholdings of those who had died. When it was all over there were more than twice the number of farmers with over fifteen acres and three times the number with more than thirty acres.

These figures are borne out by the changes in the housing stock. The numbers of 'fourth-class' houses – the one-roomed cabins which appalled so many visitors to Ireland – fell by two-thirds, while the numbers of 'first-' and 'second-class' houses increased. There were relatively few labourers left to till the land and agricultural wages showed a slight improvement. The shift from tillage to pasture accelerated. Cattle exports, which had risen steadily during the famine, continued to rise as the graziers prospered. All in all, most of the people who survived the famine were better off than they were before, not very much perhaps, but better off all the same.

Those changes bear thinking about. Nationalist visions of the famine tend to conjure up a picture of universal destitution, death and despair. The reality, as reflected in the newspapers of the time, was very different, with many people continuing to go about their business, in however subdued a manner, while the poorest sections of the community were starving all around them. There is no doubt that all levels of society did suffer, especially from diseases such as typhus and cholera which could strike down the rich as well as the poor, but for the better-off farmers there was little real deprivation; it was more a matter of laying off the farm labourers, trying to avoid paying the rates and tightening up on the family budget until the worst was over. For the poorest in society the famine meant death.

As we have seen, many of the people who suffered eviction were thrown out, not by the landlords at the top of the social pyramid, but by wealthier Catholic tenants anxious to clear their land. The same broad group, the tenant farmers, were the most rigorous in pursuing the poor people who killed their sheep or stole their turnips. Even at slightly less prosperous levels, some of those who survived may not have been altogether grieved to be able to take over a neighbour's holding. This is not to say that they sought the opportunity, or welcomed the means by which they attained greater prosperity, but very many of those who came through the dark years of the famine must have been faced, sometimes over many months, with the daily need to look after themselves and their own families, if necessary at the expense of those in greater need.

This may explain why so many survivors were extremely reticent about the famine, even many years after the worst of it was over. When collectors of folk stories tried to gather material in the early years of this century they were able to learn much more about the Great Wind of 1839, which is now just a footnote in meteorological history, than they could about the famine. The suspicion that there must have been a great deal of 'survivor guilt' is increased by the stories that have been preserved, not because they lay stress on indifference to the sufferings of others, but because, as the historian Cormac O'Grada has pointed out, they do the opposite.

The Irish Folklore Department has recorded a number of tales of miraculous rewards for human generosity during the famine. One version has the farmer being angered to see endless lines of starving people leaving his dairy with pots and pans full of milk. He goes in to berate his wife and finds all his churns as full as they were before she gave any of the milk away. Another variation has the woman giving the last of her meal to a beggar at the door and then being stricken with terror at what her husband will do when he comes home. When the man returns the meal barrel is of course full to over-flowing. The moral is not that generosity will be rewarded in Heaven, which might have been rather unsettling when so many thousands were dying all around, but here, miraculously, on Earth. What would be the point of such stories, if generosity was universal? The anonymous authors, probably priests, obviously thought that charity needed some encouragement.

There is another marked tendency in the oral tradition about the famine, and that is to minimize the death and disaster in a given area. Researchers, well aware of the vast numbers of people who died in village A, still find old people who will tell them that the suffering was not so bad in A; it was much worse in B, some miles away. The implication, of course, is that village A looked after its people and did not let them die, while village B was less generous and did. Perhaps for the same reason there are hundreds, perhaps thousands of famine graves all over Ireland, the whereabouts often known to local people, which are still unmarked and probably unconsecrated. The unmarked graves may be those of refugees from hunger in other parts of the country, or perhaps those of poor neighbours who found the doors around their homes closed against them when they contracted fever. For those living close by to admit the fact that poor people had died on their doorsteps might have implied a failure to observe the old traditions of hospitality and help to others in need. Such a failure would have been utterly understandable in the terrible conditions of the time, but might still have been a source of shame in later years.

Popular mythology is also very apt to blame 'absentee' landlords for the famine. In fact, some absentees, like the Duke of Devonshire, abated rents and did what they could to alleviate the worst sufferings of their tenants, whereas some resident landlords, such as the brutal Earl of Lucan, were completely heartless and allowed the poor to die beneath their noses. If there is any one class of landlords who behaved better than others it was those who had the money to do so. The Earl of Rosse, for instance, who had been wise enough to marry an English industrial magnate's daughter, used his wife's purse to provide work for hundreds of men, digging new water courses in the beautiful gardens of their castle, erecting miles of stone wall, excavating a moat, building a new stable block and so on, in decorative benevolence.

Some landlords remained relatively generous for the first two years of the famine and then recoiled from the vast expense of the undertaking and began to evict their tenants, just as the villains had been doing from the beginning. Among these was the Marquess of Sligo, who sold his racing cups and several paintings to help provide for the poor, and is said to have survived the famine by renting out the family box at Covent Garden Opera House. In the end he began to 'exterminate' when he realized that the British Government was never going to relieve him from the huge expense of paying the rates and providing simultaneous relief for all his smaller tenants.

Many landlords were ruined, just as the British Government intended them to be. Encumbered Estates Courts were set up specifically to deal with the bankrupt landed gentry. The law of entail was amended and the land was freed for sale. Trevelyan had expressed the hope that Protestant gentry from England and Scotland would snap up these properties. In fact many of them were bought by the lawyers who were doing the paperwork, or were sold to the new class of rich Catholic graziers. The new landlords were just as ruthless as their predecessors – more so, in fact, because some of the old gentry had been negligent, but relatively generous in allowing their estates to swarm with squatters, while the new owners cleared the land to make way for cattle and sheep.

After a generation had passed, and the surviving tenants of these landlords had recovered some confidence, many of them were ready to listen to Michael Davitt, who was himself as a child one of the victims of a famine eviction in County Mayo. Davitt took up some of the ideas pioneered by Fintan Lalor and founded the Land League. The 'Land War' of the 1880s was given surprisingly sympathetic coverage by some sections of the press, as the injustice of Irish laws governing the relationship between landlord and tenant was brought home to the English public. Even Tory politicians recognized that land reform was a pre-condition for ending violence and unrest in the Irish countryside. The

Government passed a succession of land acts during the 1890s and, by the turn of the century, the era of the great landlords was finally at an end. The big estates were broken up and the land redistributed among the small farmers. Arguably, many of these developments would have taken place whether or not the famine had occurred, but it was the heartless evictions of the famine years which first alerted the Government to the need for reform.

The Roman Catholic Church emerged from the famine with its status greatly enhanced. By 1861 there were four times as many priests, monks and nuns per thousand of the population as there had been in 1841. The erection of hundreds of new churches, which had already begun in the early years of the nineteenth century, proceeded apace. After the famine, Catholics seem to have been in special need of the consolation of their faith, and many impoverished Irish towns and villages somehow found huge sums of money to pay for the massive ecclesiastical buildings which still tower over their rooftops.

The Church of Ireland, on the other hand, never recovered from accusations of Souperism – such charges were vigorously promoted by the Roman Catholic clergy. The Established Church also had undeniably close associations with the landlord class and remained unpopular as a symbol of alien oppression. In an effort to remove this source of friction, the Government passed the Disestablishment Act in 1869, which finally toppled the Church of Ireland from its absurd position as Ireland's official religion. Many Protestants in isolated communities eventually left their homes to escape persecution, and churches where they had worshipped gradually fell into disuse and decay. Even today, the shells of abandoned Protestant churches are a familiar sight in western Ireland.

The increased veneration commanded by the Catholic Church was in some ways very much deserved. During the famine hundreds of Roman Catholic clergy died ministering to the sick and dying and many gave up the little they had to help the poor. Many priests also served on relief committees and, as we have seen, co-operated generously with other denominations. But Roman Catholic clergy were just as apt as Protestants to tell the people that the famine was a punishment for their sinful ways. And just as there were some Protestant evangelists who gave soup in exchange for souls, so there were some priests who seem to have been far more concerned to keep their flocks faithful than to keep their bellies full. To many Catholics at the time, there is no doubt that this was the right, indeed the only proper course, but if a small body of men such as the Quakers could raise some £200 000 to provide food, it is difficult to understand why the Church, with its vast international connections, could not have done more.

Was the famine mass murder, as John Mitchel maintained, or genocide, which is the word most frequently on the lips of some modern nationalists when they speak of the famine? Hardly. Even Vandeleur did not force people into gas chambers or shoot them *en masse*. To compare the Great Famine to the Jewish Holocaust, or even recent events in Rwanda, is to be deliberately misleading, both about the causes of death and the motives of the perpetrators. However, some of the specific charges levelled against the English demand closer examination.

Mitchel's insistence that there was enough home-grown food in Ireland to feed three times her population, but that the Irish people starved because it was all shipped to England, is one of the most persistent famine legends, told and re-told by thousands of people even today. The legend is untrue. The figures show that 146 000 tons of grain were exported from Ireland in 1847 compared with imports of 889 000 tons. In other words, more than six times as much grain flowed into Ireland as out of it. The excess of imports over exports continued throughout the famine, except for a crucial few months during the winter of 1846/7, before the first shiploads of maize arrived from the United States. It was only during this period, when food prices reached unprecedented levels and thousands of people were starving, that Government intervention might have been useful. On this issue the Government stands accused of failing to interfere with free trade. It was certainly guilty of the charge and would have admitted it without a blush. But it is also pertinent to ask why food – not just grain, but beef cattle, bacon, butter and cheese – was being exported in this way.

The answer, of course, is that the export of food to England and Scotland was crucial to the Irish economy then, just as it still is today. Irish farmers had depended on the English market for many years and Irish traders had made a good living out of it. Had they not done so, Ireland would have been even poorer than it was, and poverty was the root of the problem. Even if all that food had never left the country, it is highly unlikely that any of it would have reached those who needed it most, because they did not have enough money to pay for it. The wages paid on the Public Works were too low. But if they had been higher, there would have been even fewer people to till the land and prepare for the next year's crops. Even as it was, there were widespread complaints that labour was almost unobtainable because so many people were uselessly employed on the works.

In retrospect, the only measure which might have staved off disaster during that terrible winter would have been for the Government to buy up Irish farm produce at market prices and distribute as much of it as possible freely to the poor. This would have meant an enormous expenditure of public money and massive intervention in the marketplace. It would also have involved a U-turn in Government policy. Such a dramatic change of course would have led to a collision in Parliament which might well have sunk the Whigs. Naturally, they put a far higher value on their own political beliefs and their own political survival than they did on saving the lives of the Irish poor, so despite periodic hand-wringing in Parliament, they stuck to their principles and let the poor starve.

If Sir Charles Wood and Sir Charles Trevelyan (he was knighted for his services during the famine) had been intent only on saving lives, they could have brought in the soup kitchens far sooner and sustained them for longer than they did. They could have made more of the eight million pounds which they did spend immediately available as free grants, rather than as loans which everyone believed would have to be repaid. They could have maintained some form of Treasury funding for outdoor relief in distressed areas for longer and on a far more generous scale than they did. To do any of these things would have risked courting political unpopularity, because the feckless Irish were not a popular cause, and it would have incurred extra expense, which the Chancellor and his loyal civil servant were most anxious to avoid.

In view of the risks of spreading disease by bringing people together for relief, it may well be that none of these measures would have saved people's lives, but they would have demonstrated good intentions. Ironically, Trevelyan did have good intentions, but they were those of 'political economy' rather than those of simple compassion. He wanted to 'educe permanent good out of transient evil' by effecting 'a salutary revolution' in Ireland. He wanted to prevent the Irish from becoming a nation of paupers, permanently dependent on

Government hand-outs, and he proposed to do this by shifting the main support of the poor away from small-scale self-sufficiency and towards wage labour. He wanted to get rid of inefficient landlords and cumbersome laws of inheritance. He wanted to make farms viable by enlarging the size of holdings, and he honestly believed that Ireland would one day become a happier and wealthier country as a result. To some extent he succeeded, but at a terrible price.

Underlying all the controversy surrounding the failure of Government aid is the bigger issue of colonialism. The English completely failed to see, throughout the famine, that much of the behaviour which they regarded as Irish fecklessness or evasiveness, such as the widespread failure to pay the rates, was in part a resistance to what was widely regarded as an unjust tax imposed by an alien administration. We have already seen that the union between Britain and Ireland was exposed as a sham by the Great Famine. Ultimately, it was the English themselves who repudiated the union by being parsimonious with relief and introducing the 'rate-in-aid' act which insisted on Irish support for the Irish poor.

The logic of that measure was inescapable. England did not really want union enough to be prepared to pay for it. Stripped of the respectable clothing of union, the bare truth was that the English regarded Ireland as a colony, useful as a supplier of food, but full of idle, turbulent and racially inferior people, who might be helped a little if the need arose, but not at too great a cost. Contemporary political cartoons reveal this attitude all too clearly. In these circumstances it is not in the least surprising that many Irish people with dignity and spirit regarded British rule as intolerable and were willing to bend the truth a little if it helped to get rid of them. In this context, Mitchel's accusations of genocide make sound political sense.

Does it matter if some stories – indeed some recent books – about the famine are still grossly exaggerated? I believe it does. The facts of British misrule and mismanagement during the famine are bad enough. Embellishing them only obscures the truth and makes it impossible to learn anything from the whole sad business. Wild stories which fail to stand up to stringent examination also give ammunition to the cynics and apologists for colonial rule, who would like to believe that the famine never happened. The long struggle for independence may have justified the need for propaganda, without being too pernickety about the facts, but today the need is for reconciliation and this depends on accepting the whole truth and not just those bits that incite a desire for vengeance.

At the same time, it is possible to take an old myth and put it to new use. Some legends may not be strictly true, but they have a symbolic value which serves to focus people's minds on other problems. There is a story from the west of Ireland which illustrates this very well. It concerns a group of 600 starving people who gathered in Louisburgh, County Mayo, in the early spring of 1847 to seek food from the relieving officer. According to the story, the official said that he had nothing for them and they must go and see the guardians, who were lunching the following day at Delphi, a quaintly named fishing lodge belonging to the Marquess of Sligo, on the far side of Doo Lough, the Black Lake.

The road to Delphi was long and hard, ten miles of rough going across a great bog and then up through a mountain pass and finally alongside the darkly brooding waters of the lake. The weather was cold and wet and the people were weak from hunger. At one point the path ran through a river, swollen with flood. Some of the poor people are said to have drowned at that point and others died of cold and exhaustion along the way. At last they reached the lodge and waited, patiently, until the Guardians had finished their ample lunch. They then made a desperate appeal for food to relieve their hunger. The Guardians sent them away, empty-handed, and the starving people were obliged to make the long, dangerous return journey along the steep and rocky path which ran alongside the lough.

In 1918 the story was put into writing by a local journalist, James Berry, who wrote a highly-coloured account of the tragedy sixty-one years after it was supposed to have happened. In appalling weather, weak from lack of food, the people began to die along the path above Doo Lough:

> It was a deliberate trap, set up by the Government … to decoy the starving Celts out into this wild region in order to slaughter them … when they reached that terrible spot called the Stroppabue, on the very brow of the cliff, the tremendous squalls swept them by the score into the lake …

There are plenty of local people who will swear to the truth of the story of the people being blown into the lake like so many dead leaves. Some say that 400 people drowned in the tragedy; some say 600. One remarkable version, which appeared recently in the London *Independent,* upped the numbers involved to 20 000. The facts are rather different. If the walk to Delphi did take place it was in 1849, not 1847, when a report of six deaths by drowning in Doo Lough appeared in a local newspaper. The individuals were named and the names of their townlands were also given. It is possible that there were more deaths, perhaps as many as ten, or even twelve. The cleft among the rocks where they are supposed to be buried hardly has room for more. There was a relieving officer in Louisburgh at the time and it is entirely possible that the Guardians could have lunched at Delphi and that several starving people went to beg help from them and perished on the journey. As so often with legends of this kind, there is a small core of truth. All the rest is fiction.

What seems to have happened is that James Berry heard about the tragedy, perhaps already inflated by local legend, embellished it a bit more and added a few political flourishes. As nationalist propaganda it did a very good job and, in 1918, with the struggle for independence at its height, he may well have seen a need for it. But the use that has been made of the story in recent years has a different agenda. Don Mullan, director of an Irish charity called Afri, heard about the legend of Doo Lough and thought that a walk along the route from Louisburgh to Delphi would be an excellent way of focusing people's minds on the hunger and suffering which still endures in many poor countries of the world. Within a few years he had made the walk an annual event, which now attracts well-wishers from all over Ireland to come to Louisburgh one Saturday in May and remember the poor of the world as they retrace the path alongside Doo Lough.

Today's walkers are aware that the scale of the Doo Lough tragedy is in doubt, but they do not doubt the scale of the tragedy of the Great Famine, of which this story is only a symbol. The walk is also a symbolic act, not an exercise in historical statistics, and as such it commands respect. It also serves to draw the attention of many more people to the desperate situation of the world's poor, who still suffer so many of the disadvantages that the poor Irish suffered in the Great Famine.

The parallels must not be pushed too hard because every situation is different, but there are many parts of the world today where people are in constant danger of starvation, partly because rich individuals or big companies are hogging the best land and a growing population of poor people is pushed out on to the margins, where life is increasingly precarious. Like the Irish in the 1840s, these poor farmers are dependent on the success of a staple crop which is liable to failure when weather conditions are unsuitable or there is some other unforeseen catastrophe. The Ethiopian famines of 1983 and 1984 were caused by drought, not plant disease, but the dependence on the success of a single crop was analogous to the Irish situation, as were the famine diseases of dysentery, typhus and relapsing fever from which so many of the people died.

Other examples are not hard to find. The poor people of Bangladesh suffer from famine when their smallholdings are drowned beneath the waters of the Ganges, but they would not even be living on the swampy delta islands if they had free access to safer places on dry land. There are many other places in Africa, or elsewhere on the Indian sub-continent, where the poor have multiplied in numbers and have been forced to try and make a living by subsistence agriculture on land which can only support them as long as the political situation is stable and the climate remains favourable. As in nineteenth-century Ireland there is no margin for failure. And as in nineteenth-century Ireland, there is often an elite, sometimes an alien elite, who exploit the misery of the poor and ignore their sufferings.

We ourselves, all of us, play a part in this process without intending to do so. Many poor countries are locked into debt repayments which force them to try and maximize the return from cash crops for export in order to earn hard currency to service the debt. The best land is taken for cotton, or cocoa, or coffee or some other commodity which is in demand in richer countries. Competition in the international marketplace keeps the prices for these products low and forces down living standards for the growers, so that we can have cheap food and cheap clothing. Concentration on cash crops contributes to the problems of the subsistence farmers, who must make do with the poorest land to grow their crops and who often even lack the alternative of low-paid casual labour on the plantations. In a sense, though it would not do to strain the

point, we are the absentee landlords and the poorest of the world's people are the famine Irish of today.

The recently opened Famine Museum at Strokestown Park in County Roscommon, where the landlord Denis Mahon was murdered, draws these parallels and makes the visitor think about them.

The curator, Luke Dodd, believes that one of the reasons why today's Irish give so generously to Third World causes is because they have experienced colonial exploitation and been through the trauma of the famine. When the museum was opened in 1994, the President of the Irish Republic, Mary Robinson, enlarged on this point:

> We are a reasonably prosperous country, but our experience has been that of a colony striving for our independence and of a country devastated by appalling famine, and that is part of our subconscious. It has been something which … gives us a particular understanding of developing countries. I think we have that, and I think that's one of the reasons why Irish people, priests, nuns, aid workers, teachers, work in developing countries and do it the right way, with a commitment to empowering, helping, building up the strengths of the communities they work with.

President Robinson has demonstrated that she cares about the world's poor. Alone among the world's leaders, she herself went to visit the relief centres in Somalia in 1992, where, at great risk to themselves, workers from the Irish charity Concern fed thousands of starving people, while soldiers fighting under the flag of the United Nations waged a futile and expensive war against elusive clan leaders. Unfortunately, the Irish President has little power even over politicians of her own country. On the world stage hers is a moral authority, no more.

Victims of modern famine: mother and children in Ethiopia.
The victims may be different, but Trevelyan's market forces still
govern the relationship between rich and poor.

Mary Robinson, President of the Irish Republic, at the official opening of the Strokestown famine museum in 1994.

At the time of the famine, efforts to relieve the people were hindered, as we have seen, by blind adherence to economic dogma. Today, the wheel of economic philosophy has come full circle. Right-wing politicians almost everywhere endorse Trevelyan's beliefs in the evils of government subsidy and the need for the profit motive in the marketplace as if they too were privy to Divine revelation. To hear them speak, one might imagine that the Great Famine had never happened, the limitations of this kind of thinking never exposed. The intractable problems with which the world is faced today are going to need far more radical solutions.

Market forces are not going to counter the threat of global warming, or stop the felling of the forests, or slow down the expansion of the world's deserts. Still less are they likely to provide a solution to the growing disparity between the world's rich and the world's poor. We do not have to be possessed of second sight to know that famine will return to Somalia, or Ethiopia, or some other poor country, and that western politicians will once again be taken by surprise and despatch too little aid too late to save the lives of thousands of people. Perhaps, like the English politicians of the mid-nineteenth century, they have other priorities. And perhaps we ourselves, who elect them to office, do not really care enough to make them think otherwise.

SELECT BIBLIOGRAPHY

Bardon, Jonathan, *A History of Ulster*, Belfast 1992

Bourke, Austin, *The Visitation of God? The Potato and the Great Irish Famine*, ed. Hill and O'Grada, Dublin 1993

Bowen, Desmond, *Souperism, Myth or Reality?*, London 1963

Crawford, E. Margaret (ed.), *Famine – The Irish Experience*, Edinburgh 1989

Cushing, J. Elizabeth (ed.), *A Chronicle of Irish Emigration to Saint John, New Brunswick 1847*, Saint John 1979

Daly, Mary E., *The Famine in Ireland*, Dublin 1986

Davis, Richard, *William Smith O'Brien, Ireland 1848*, Dublin 1989

Donnelly, James S. Jr., *The Land and the People of Nineteenth Century Cork*, London 1975

Edwards, R. Dudley, and Williams, T. Desmond. (eds.), *The Great Famine, Studies in Irish History, 1845-52*, Dublin 1956

Foster, R. S. (ed.), *The Oxford History of Ireland*, London 1989

Hickey, Patrick, 'Famine, Mortality and Emigration, a profile of six parishes 1846-47', *Cork History and Society*, Dublin 1993

Hill, Lord George, *Facts from Gweedore*, London 1845, reprinted 1887, facsimile ed. Belfast 1971

Kinealy, Christine, *This Great Calamity, The Irish Famine 1845-52*, Dublin 1994

Lyons, F. S. L., *Ireland Since the Famine*, London 1971

Miller, Kerby A., *Emigrants and Exiles, Ireland and the Irish Exodus to North America*, Oxford 1985

Mitchel, John, *The History of Ireland*, London and Dublin 1869

Mokyr, Joel, *Why Ireland Starved: A Quantitative and Analytical History of the Irish Economy*, London 1985

Murphy, Fr. Ignatius, 'The Parish of Kilfearagh and its People, 1834-1851', Killaloe Diocesan Archives, unpublished

Nicholson, Asenath, *Ireland's Welcome to a Stranger*, London 1847

Nicholson, Asenath, *Lights and Shades of Ireland*, London 1850

O'Gallagher, Marianna, *Grosse Ile, Gateway to Canada*, Quebec 1984

O'Gallchochbair, Proinnsias, *History of Landlordism in Donegal*, Ballyshannon 1962

O'Grada, Cormac, *Ireland Before and After the Famine*, Manchester 1988

O'Grada, Cormac, *The Great Irish Famine*, Dublin 1989

O'Rourke, Canon John, *The Great Irish Famine*, Dublin 1874, reprinted 1989

O' Tuathaigh, Gearoid, *Ireland before the Famine*, Dublin 1972

Salaman, Redcliffe, *The History and Social Influence of the Potato*, ed. Hawkes, Cambridge 1985

Smith, Elizabeth, *Irish Journals 1840-1850*, ed. Thomas and McGusty, Oxford 1980

Toner, P. M. (ed.), *New Ireland Remembered*, Fredericton 1989

Trevelyan, Charles, 'The Irish Crisis', *Edinburgh Review* 1848

Woodham-Smith, Cecil, *The Great Hunger, Ireland 1845-1849*, London 1962

Young, Arthur, *A Tour in Ireland, 1776-1779*, 2 vols, ed. Hutton, London 1892

NOTES

Full bibliographical details, if not given here, can be found in the Select Bibliography

19 'nits breed lice': Bardon, p138
'It hath pleased God': quoted in Taylor Downing (ed.), *The Troubles*, London 1980, p13

21 Penal Laws: Bardon, p168

26 ramshackle pyramid: Bourke, p58
so-called middlemen: Daly, pp14-15
sub-division: Salaman, p191

28 Little of this investment: O' Tuathaigh, p144
relative prosperity: Foster, p147

29 volunteer militia: ibid., p149
Presbyterian radicals: ibid., p151

33 price of grain: Mokyr, pp280-1

35 widespread use: Salaman, p222-4

36 slightly taller: O'Grada, *Ireland Before and After the Famine*, p21
conacre rents: Bourke, p59

37 ten pounds an acre: Donnelly, p20

38 store the food value: Bourke, p54

39 always in want: Sir John Burgoyne, *The Times*, 6 Oct. 1847
'The extension of': quoted in Trevelyan, p230

42 'The population': speech by the Earl of Rosse to Parsonstown union farmers, 1843
Duke of Wellington: Trevelyan, p237

'The proper business': ibid., p315

44 full employment: O'Grada, *Ireland Before and After the Famine*, p17
Ulster custom: Bardon, p178

50 *clachans ... rundale*: Hill, p22
boulay (bouley): E. Estyn Evans, *Irish Heritage*, 1919, p47
McKye (M'Kye) letter: Hill, pp9-10

51 arrears with their rent: ibid., p18
not a shortage of land: ibid., p22

52 set up a store: ibid., pp36-40
pleasure people feel: ibid., p42

53 Protestant church: O'Gallchochbair, p27
£472 to a total of £1100: ibid., p27
organizing relief: Kinealy, p126

55 *Evening Post:* Bourke, pp142-8
constabulary: Relief Commission papers, INA Z17152, National Archives, Dublin

56 'The potato failure': Smith
fungus infection: Bourke, pp150-8

58 avert disaster: Woodham-Smith, pp55-6
'Peel's Brimstone': Trevelyan p249

62 Sir Charles Wood: Woodham-Smith, p87
'On the 27th': quoted in Trevelyan, p246

63 'The first alarm': ibid., p247

66 serious riots: Woodham-Smith, p125

67 stopped exports: Miller, p286

68 scurvy: Edwards and Williams, p269

69 deaths from starvation: Trevelyan, p257
'swollen to twice their size': Donnelly, p85

70 'a person will live': Nicholson, *Lights and Shades of Ireland*
'although a man': quoted in Woodham-Smith, pp154-5

71 Confrontations between mobs: Donnelly, pp89-91
A Cork magistrate: ibid., p87

73 'It wasn't tilling': quoted in Murphy, p206

76 notorious recipe: quoted in Salaman, p311

77 Evangelical movement: Bowen, pp88-105

81 'What is the object': *Achill Missionary Herald,* 22 August 1846
'I give you my advice': quoted in letter from Nangle to Lord Morpeth, 18 October 1838, Collection of John O'Shea, Achill Island

83 'I had looked': Nicholson, *Ireland's Welcome to a Stranger*

84 priest and parson: Bowen, pp88-105

85 Robert Traill: Hickey, pp880-7
Caffin: ibid., p883

87 total of 750 000: Trevelyan, pp256-7
fever: Edwards and Williams, pp265-8

89 'Six men': Nicholson, *Lights and Shades of Ireland*

90 Lowtherstown: NI Public Records Office BGXV/A/2, Belfast

91 three million people: Trevelyan, p269

93 'all-merciful Providence': ibid., p320
Marshall: Hickey, pp889-903

95 'A large population': Trevelyan, p303

98 Major Denis Mahon: Strokestown Famine papers, National Famine Museum, Strokestown Park

101 Mr Walshe: Woodham-Smith, pp319-20

102 'The admission': quoted in Murphy, p227

104 Osborne, Sidney Godolphin, *Gleanings from the West of Ireland,* London 1850

105 'I can tell you': quoted in Murphy, p221

107 pig slaughterhouse: ibid., p231

108 'It insists upon': *Illustrated London News* Vol. XII, No. 324

110 'We who preach': *The Nation,* 10 July 1847

112 'My remedy': *The Nation,* 15 July 1848

115 isolated farmhouse: *Illustrated London News,* 12 August 1848, p90

117 'Whole districts': *Tipperary Vindicator,* 6 December 1848

120 300 000 Irish people: Trevelyan, pp291-2

125 slightly more prosperous: Edwards and Williams, p321
bolted with the money: ibid., p326

128 the slave ships: P. Edwards (ed.), *Equiano's Travels,* London 1967, pp25-30

131 Grosse Ile: O'Gallagher, pp50-8

134 German immigrants: Edwards and Williams, pp366-7

135 Moses Perley: Provincial Archives New Brunswick (PANB) P8/236
In his report: PANB RG3 RS 555 B/5

136 'to relieve the estates': PANB RG3 RS 555 E/9
longing to return: Miller, p316

137 'There are many': PANB RG3 RS 555 A/7

138 acknowledging their debt: Cushing, p50

142 coped very well: Miller, pp313-14

143 'The passengers were': *The Nation,* 3 July 1847

146 lunatic asylum: Miller, p320
select committee: Report on Tenant Houses, State of New York 205, New York Public Library, New York 1857
'far exceeded': ibid. p3

147 'reckless slovenliness': ibid., pp13-14

152 'Now those 1 500 000 men': Mitchel, p459

153 unsavoury career: Lyons, p109

156 'Last night at ten': Dublin *News Letter,* 7 March 1867

157 'Between 1172 and 1867': *The Nation,* 9 March 1867

167 'I gladly share': *Illustrated London News,* 11 August 1849, p90
'The mutual satisfaction': *Illustrated London News* 11 August 1849

171 birthrates also fell: Hickey, pp896-7

172 Overall figures: Mokyr, pp264-8
size of the farms: O'Tuathaigh, p206

174 Catholic tenants: Miller, p288

178 The figures show: Bourke, p169

179 sunk the Whigs: O'Tuathaigh, p219

INDEX

PICTURE CREDITS

BBC Books would like to thank the following for providing photographs and for permission to reproduce copyright material. While every effort has been made to trace and acknowledge all copyright holders, we would like to apologize should there have been any errors or omissions.

Abbreviations: HDC=Hulton Deutsch Collection; NLI=The National Library of Ireland, Dublin; ILN=*The Illustrated London News* Picture Library.

Page 12, HDC; 14, The Board of Trinity College, Dublin; 17, By Courtesy of The National Portrait Gallery, London; 18, The Ashmolean Museum, Oxford; 20, NLI; 21, HDC; 22, The National Gallery of Ireland, Dublin; 24-25, The Famine Museum, Strokestown, Co. Roscommon; 30, NLI; 34, 40-1, 43, The Ulster Museum, Belfast; 47, The Irish Architectural Archive, Dublin; 51, NLI; 54, ILN, 22.12.1849; 57, ILN, 29.8.1846, p.133; 59 (inset), By Courtesy of The Reform Club; 59, By Courtesy of The National Portrait Gallery, London; 65 (left & right below), HDC; (right above), By Courtesy of The National Portrait Gallery, London; 69, NLI; 72, Rural History Centre, University of Reading, Berkshire; 74, ILN, 16.1.1847, p.44; 78, Sean Sexton Collection, London; 79 (inset), Courtesy of Violet McDowell; 79 & 82-3 NLI; 86 (above), Father Patrick Hickey; 86, ILN, 13.2.1847, p.101; 94, ILN, 16.12.1848, p.380; 99, The Famine Museum, Strokestown, Co. Roscommon; 102, NLI; 103 & 106, Sean Sexton Collection, London; 110, HDC; 111, Punch, Vol II (July-December 1846), p.79; 115, ILN, 12.8.1848 (cover); 116, ILN, 12.8.1848, p.92; 118, HDC; 121, Mary Evans Picture Library; 122-23, Sean Sexton Collection, London; 124, Liverpol Libraries and Information Service; 129, Mary Evans Picture Library; 130, 137 & 140, HDC; 145, 149, 151 & 155, Range/Bettmann; 157, ILN, 28.9.1867, p.340; 160, Range/Bettmann; 162, Collections/Brian Shuel, London; 165, Punch, Vol.16 (January-June 1849) p.79; 168, ILN, 22.12.1849, p.404; 169, ILN, 18.8.1849, p.125; 173, Sean Sexton Collection, London; 184, © Bridie Russell/Oxfam; 186, The Famine Museum, Strokestown, Co. Roscommon.

Colour Section, between pp96 & 97
1, 2 & 5, Department of Irish Folklore, University College, Dublin; 3, National Gallery of Scotland, Edinburgh; 4, NLI; 6, National Archives of Canada, Ottowa.